THE CHRISTIAN
TRAVELER'S
GUIDE
to the Holy Land

THE CHRISTIAN
TRAVELER'S
GUIDE
to the Holy Land

Charles H. Dyer and Gregory A. Hatteberg

BROADMAN
&HOLMAN
PUBLISHERS

Nashville, Tennessee

©1998
by Charles H. Dyer and Greg Hatteberg
All rights reserved
Printed in the United States of America
0-8054-0156-3
Published by Broadman & Holman Publishers, Nashville, Tennessee
Dewey Decimal Classification: 915.69
Subject Heading: HOLYLAND-GUIDEBOOKS
Library of Congress Card Catalog Number: 97-44785
Page Design by Anderson Thomas Design
Typography by TF Designs, Mt. Juliet, Tennessee

Photograph Credits

Arnold, Nancy, pp. 57; 58, top; 185, bottom; 187, bottom; 190; 192; 197, top right.

Biblical Illustrator, Nashville, Tenn. (David Rogers), pp. 72; 166; 182.

Biblical Illustrator, Nashville, Tenn. (Ken Touchton), pp. 55, middle; 70; 87; 107; 120; 169; 170, bottom; 172, middle and bottom; 174; 175, top; 180, top; 181, bottom; 185, top; 186, top; 188, middle; 196, middle right.

Brisco, Thomas, pp. 112; 118; 176, middle; 181, top; 183, top; 184, top; 191, bottom; 195; 197, top left.

Dyer, Charlie and Greg Hatteberg, pp. 47; 49; 55, bottom; 56; 63; 74; 76; 109; 114; 126; 129; 131; 156; 168, top; 171, top; 173, top and bottom; 175, bottom; 176, top; 177, top; 179, top and bottom; 184, middle; 186, bottom; 188, top and bottom; 194, middle and bottom; 196, middle left and bottom.

Ellis, C. Randolph, pp. 103; 170, top; 172, top; 180, bottom; 193, bottom.

Langston, Scot, pp. 44; 58, bottom; 59; 64; 85, top; 89; 105; 191, top; 193, top and middle; 194, top; 197, middle.

Scofield Collection, Dargan Research Library, Nashville, Tenn., pp. 116; 146; 147; 177, bottom; 179, middle; 184, bottom; 187, top; 196, top; 197, bottom left.

Smith, Marsha Ellis, p. 153.

Southwestern Baptist Theological Seminary, A. Webb Roberts Library, p. 121.

Stephens, Bill, pp. 171, bottom; 183, bottom.

Tolar, William B., pp. 78; 79; 83; 85, bottom; 135; 136; 168, bottom; 176, bottom; 189, top and bottom.

Map Credits

Broadman & Holman Publishers ©1998, pp. 37; 38; 167; 178; 198.

Dedication

This book is lovingly dedicated to our wives
Kathy Dyer and Lisa Hatteberg
who share our love for the lands of the Bible.

"Many women do noble things, but you surpass
them all" (Prov. 31:29).

Table of Contents

TABLE of CONTENTS

Introduction

Knowing the land of the Bible is as important to understanding God's Word as knowing the layout of a baseball diamond is to comprehending the game of baseball! Imagine explaining a baseball game to a friend from another culture who had never seen, or played, the sport.

You casually mention the baseball diamond, and your listener pictures a small stone dangling from a necklace. You excitedly describe a close play at second base while your friend wonders how many bases the ball controls . . . and if the bases are heavily guarded. You cheer when the manager summons the ace reliever from the bull pen while your bewildered companion envisions a victorious matador striding from a pen of bulls.

You can laugh at the analogy, but we all do something similar when we read the Bible. We hear the story of Gideon choosing his three hundred men by the spring of Harod, and we substitute our own image of the event. Some picture a small stream thirty feet wide while others see a broad river hundreds of feet across. Some imagine the water rushing down a steep mountainside while others envision it meandering across flat plains.

The problem is that in many cases, our own images cloud the biblical account and make it harder to understand. What makes perfect sense to someone standing at the spot where it happened seems almost incomprehensible to someone who has never been to the Holy Land and who reads the account knowing only the geography of Pennsylvania, Illinois, or Texas.

Traveling to Israel helps an individual view the Bible through a new set of geographical lenses. Simple phrases like "going up to Jerusalem" jump off the pages of God's Word because they now make sense. Capernaum becomes more than just a name on a page. Israel's temptation in the wilderness comes alive when your feet stumble over the desert rocks and your water bottle starts to run dry.

God chose this land to teach His people specific lessons of faith. But why would God choose for His people a land of marginal climate that was coveted by larger surrounding nations? Jim Monson has offered a provocative explanation for God's choice.

> In all of these biblical periods this land served as God's testing ground of faith. It was here, in this land where both personal and national existence was threatened, that Israel's leaders and people were called upon to learn the true meaning of security and well-being, of trust in the Lord their God. It was here that God's weakness was shown to be stronger than men (James M. Monson, *The Land Between: A Regional Study Guide to the Land of the Bible* [Jerusalem: By the author, 1983],14).

If you are reading this book in preparation for a trip to Israel, congratulations! You are about to take a journey that will make a profound spiritual impact on your life. You will soon traverse a land where God actively intervened in the lives of men and women . . . a land where the incarnate Son of God taught, healed, died for your sins, and rose from the dead. You will return a different person.

We suggest you read chapter 1, "Preparing for the Trip," as soon as possible. In that section we offer specific information to help you prepare physically and spiritually for this journey of a lifetime. Once you know your final itinerary, begin reading the information on the specific sites you will visit. This will prepare you to gain as much information as possible from your trip. During your tour, keep this book with you as a handy guide . . . and as a convenient place to take notes, record pictures, and write your impressions. These records will be invaluable to you as you return home.

Our prayer for you is that this journey to the places of the Bible will make as profound an impact on your life as it has made on ours.

INTRODUCTION

Go with an open, receptive heart and ask God to give you a sense of wonderment, awe, and excitement as you "walk through the length and breadth of the land" (Gen. 13:17).

Section One

Preparing for the Trip

Israel Travel Safety Facts

Tips for Travelers

Packing List

Conversational Hebrew and Arabic

How to Overcome Jet Lag

Requirements for Obtaining a U.S. Passport

A Four-Week Schedule of
Bible Reading and Prayer to Prepare for Israel

A Four-Week Bible Series to
Prepare a Group Spiritually for a Trip to Israel

Israel Travel Safety Facts

1. Airport security for all flights going into Israel is very thorough.

2. Tel Aviv's Ben Gurion International Airport is recognized by the world at large as the most security-conscious airport in the world.

3. Terrorists have not targeted American tourists within Israel.

4. Never in the history of Israel have Americans been evacuated.

5. One is in more danger of death or injury driving from his or her home to the airport than of being attacked by terrorists while in Israel.

6. Several steps can be taken to minimize even further one's chances of being involved in terrorist incidents:

   a. Avoid wearing articles of clothing that advertise your nationality or actively identify you with one side or the other in the current Middle East conflict.

   b. Avoid those countries that have proven to be havens for terrorists and terrorist activities.

   c. Travel in a group and avoid those areas that are prone to unrest (similar to the advice you would give someone coming to visit any major city in the United States).

7. Tour buses are in constant contact with their headquarters. The tour operators monitor any potential trouble spots; and if they feel there might be a problem, they will contact the driver and reroute the group to avoid the area.

"Israel is a country of great beauty, awesome history . . . and peaceful serenity. All of which is revered and protected by the best international security system of a free society in the world."

—Captain Tom Ashwood, security chief,
U.S. Airline Pilots Association

Tips for Travelers

CLOTHING

Israel is very informal. You will have no real dress-up occasions, even for Sunday. For touring, plan to wear comfortable clothes. Most tours encourage participants to wear jeans, slacks, or shorts on the trip. Dresses for ladies and jackets and ties for men are optional for evening wear and are usually not required. Take one jacket or heavy sweater, even during the summer months.

Remember when packing: Less is better. Comfortable shoes with nonskid soles are necessary. You will be doing a great deal of walking, often over uneven terrain and smooth stones. Wash-and-wear items are very helpful; and shorts are acceptable. However, those who wear shorts should also carry a "modesty kit" for visiting holy sites or traveling in Arab or conservative Jewish areas. A modesty kit for women should include slacks or a wrap-around skirt (below the knee), a blouse that covers the shoulders, and a hat or scarf for the head. A modesty kit for men should include long pants and a shirt that covers the shoulders. Carry your modesty kit with you on the bus and ask your guide when to wear it.

CURRENCY

Depending on what is covered in your tour, extra expenses may include incidental food items such as beverages, snacks, and lunch. You will also want to bring money to purchase souvenirs. Of that amount, you should carry at least $25.00 in one dollar bills with the rest in cash or U.S. traveler's checks. (The one dollar bills can be used to purchase items such as bottled water, soft drinks, and postcards.) You can exchange dollars into the local currency at airports, hotels, and banks. Whenever you exchange dollars, keep the receipt given to you. You will then be able to convert any remaining currency back into dollars when you leave the country. Most stores love U.S. dollars, but you can sometimes get better bargains if you pay in the local currency.

The basic unit of money in Israel is the New Israeli Shekel (NIS) which is divided into one hundred Agorot. Check the foreign currency exchange section in your local newspaper to determine the current exchange rate just before you leave on your trip.

You should consider the use of a money belt. Clever pickpockets are waiting for you. Carry and guard your passport, pocketbook, purse, and other valuables very carefully. Keep your money, traveler's checks, and passport on your person or in your hotel safe deposit box. Never pack them in your luggage or leave them in your hotel room. Larger purchases can be made using a major credit card, but go through your wallet or purse before leaving the United States to remove all unnecessary credit cards (just in case your wallet is lost or stolen).

ELECTRIC APPLIANCES

The electric current in Israel is 220-volt A.C., single phase, 50 cycles which requires special adapter plugs with round prongs. If you intend to take appliances (hair dryer, electric razor, iron) that are suitable for both 110 and 220 volts, make sure to carry a set of adapter plugs. If your appliance is for 110 volts only, you will also need a converter. Never plug your 110-volt appliance into a 220-volt outlet without a converter; it will work at twice its speed for a few seconds—and never work again!

HEALTH

You do not need shots or vaccinations to visit Israel. However, should you need any medication, be sure to carry it with you. Also, take some of the following items along for any emergencies: diarrhea medicine (liquid or tablets), sleeping pills (to help overcome jet lag the first few nights), motion sickness medication (if you are subject to motion sickness), cold or allergy tablets (if you are subject to allergy attacks), and any other personal hygiene products you may require.

LUGGAGE

International airlines normally limit passengers to one large piece of luggage and one carry-on bag (excluding purse or camera bag). In addition to satisfying airline regulations, this limitation also makes it much easier for individuals to keep track of their luggage when it is being loaded and unloaded from the buses and when it is portered at hotels. Be sure your suitcase closes and fastens securely (use extra straps if necessary). Mark your suitcase and carry-on bag clearly so you will be able to distinguish them. Women should consider using only their initials rather than their first names. Do not pack cameras, expensive jewelry, or other valuables in your luggage. Keep these with you in your hand luggage.

Be sure to pack anything you will need on the flight in your carry-on bag. Also keep your essential toiletries and a one-day change of clothes with you in your carry-on luggage—just in case your suitcase should get "lost in transit." Don't overpack. Save some room for items you may purchase and bring back. Remember that on the way over, you will be wearing the same clothes for two days—walking, riding, and sleeping in airplanes. Dress for comfort!

MEALS

Hotels serve nutritious breakfasts in Israel, so don't skip breakfast! Lunches may or may not be included in your tour. (Check with your travel agent.) Dinner will be ample. Some foods will be new to you. Any foods served at the hotels will usually be safe to eat. Exercise care in eating unpeeled fruit and fresh vegetables purchased in open-air markets unless you peel and/or wash them first. Consider bringing along some snack foods to eat on the bus when you are traveling.

Tap water in Israel is safe. Coffee, tea, soft drinks, and bottled water are also safe to drink. Sometimes the coffee is very strong. Order "filtered coffee" if you want normal coffee. Before you order other drinks at meals, check to see if they are included in the price of your tour. Usually you are required to pay for any extra drinks you order with meals.

OTHER ITEMS TO PACK

Consider packing a washcloth, wash-n-dries for warm touring days, and your own soap—if it is important to you. Don't forget your sunglasses, and remember that a hat is an absolute necessity. (One with a broad brim is a wise choice.) Bring your bathing suit if you want to try your hand at swimming in the Mediterranean Sea, Dead Sea, or Sea of Galilee. You can request a wake-up call from the hotel switchboard, but you may also want to carry a portable alarm clock. Boxed snacks (dried fruit, etc.) can help keep your energy up between meals. Any liquids you take should be in tight (preferably plastic) bottles. Only fill them three-fourths full to allow for expansion. Put each bottle in a small plastic zip-lock bag for further protection.

PASSPORT INFORMATION

Make sure your passport is up to date. No visas are necessary for individuals with U.S., Canadian, or British passports. Keep your passport with you at all times. Also, keep a separate record of your passport number. The easiest way to do this is to make a photocopy of your passport and pack the photocopy in your luggage. Do not pack your passport when traveling! Carry it with you in a safe place at all times.

If you plan to travel to Moslem countries other than Egypt, Jordan, or Turkey, on arrival in Israel ask the passport control officer not to stamp your passport. (You cannot visit some Moslem countries with an Israeli-stamped passport.) As you hand over your passport, just say, "Please do not stamp my passport." The officer will issue you a separate temporary visa. Keep this with your passport at all times. It will be removed when you leave Israel.

PHOTOGRAPHY

Take a camera and plenty of film. (Film is expensive overseas.) Also, take an extra set of batteries for your camera. You may wish to invest in a lead-lined bag to hold your film to avoid any X ray damage. (Film can be hand inspected in U.S. airports, but European and Israeli inspectors will run it through their X ray machines.) You may be required to unload your camera for inspection when boarding planes. Sometimes they will permit you to snap a blank picture instead of removing the roll, but you cannot count on this. The best policy is to make sure you have no film in your camera when you arrive at the airport.

If you have a new, expensive foreign camera, you may wish to register it with U.S. Customs at the airport before leaving the United States. Otherwise, you might be charged duty on it when coming back into the United States. (Your valid sales slip will be proof instead, if you prefer.)

Take a small cassette recorder (or use the photography section in this book) to keep a record of each picture as soon as you take it. Later you will not recognize all you took during the trip. Use discretion in what you photograph—especially military personnel and installations, Moslem women with covered faces, orthodox Jews, etc. When in doubt, ask permission first.

PHYSICAL EXERCISE

Israel is a land of hills and valleys, and you will be walking up and down many of them. It is strongly recommended that you begin walking early to condition yourself. You may want to use the shoes you plan to wear in Israel just so they are "broken in," and you are comfortable walking in them.

SHOPPING

The English language is spoken sufficiently everywhere so that language is never a problem. Shopping is fun in Israel, but be careful with your money. Sometimes street peddlers and shops charge much for things of little worth. Don't feel pressured to buy. Part of the fun in shopping is the Middle Eastern custom of "bargaining" for an item. When bargaining with the peddlers, never accept the first price of an item as the actual price. Usually the item can be purchased for less than half of the "asking price." (Read Proverbs 20:14 before you go shopping!) Keep a record of all your purchases as this will make the filing of your customs report easy. Be careful about exposing much money at any one time.

TELEPHONE

Calls to the United States can be placed through the switchboard at all hotels. However, most hotels add a service charge for this service. If you have a telephone company credit card, you can make a direct call through the appropriate international operator and avoid the hotel surcharge. The numbers for the three major long-distance carriers are as follows:

AT&T USA Direct	177-100-2727
MCI Call USA	177-150-2727
US SPRINT Sprint Express	177-102-2727

If you are using a different long-distance company, check with them before you depart to see if they have an international operator number for Israel.

TRAVELING AS PART OF A GROUP

Sometimes photographers will take pictures of you or your group. These pictures make a lovely souvenir of the trip, but you are not obligated to buy any. Expect some inconveniences such as schedule changes. Things do not always run as smoothly as they do in the United States.

Be careful about sharing your faith. This is an especially sensitive situation. Let your life and conduct count. Consider the believers there whose situation you might make more difficult by arousing anger or by giving a poor testimony.

Pray for the tour. Live with others as Christians. Plan to cooperate and stay on schedule with the group. The guide and tour host are concerned for the welfare of the entire group, and they count on your cooperation to make it an enjoyable time for all.

WEATHER

Winter weather in Israel is very changeable, and November through March is the rainy season. While you should have some beautiful days, expect to see rain, especially in the hill country. The average temperature can vary greatly depending on where you are in Israel. Expect cool days and cold nights in Jerusalem. Following are the average high/low temperatures for various spots in Israel in the winter.

	Nov.	Dec.	Jan.	Feb.	Mar.
Jerusalem	67/54	56/47	53/43	57/44	61/47
Tel Aviv	76/54	66/47	65/49	66/48	69/51
Sea of Galilee	78/59	68/53	65/48	67/49	72/51
Dead Sea	83/61	74/51	70/49	73/51	79/56

Spring and summer weather is very stable and pleasant. April and May can still see occasional rain, but little or no rain will fall from June through October. The average summer temperature can still vary greatly. Expect warm days and cool nights in Jerusalem. The following are the average high/low temperatures for various spots in Israel in the summer.

	Apr.	May	June	July	Aug.
Jerusalem	69/53	77/60	81/63	84/66	86/66
Tel Aviv	72/54	77/63	83/67	86/70	86/72
Sea of Galilee	80/56	89/62	95/68	98/73	99/75
Dead Sea	87/63	95/69	99/75	103/77	104/79

Packing List

The following list is intended to help you pack more efficiently. If you have any special needs, be sure to add those items to your list. Items with an asterisk (*) may be optional.

CLOTHING

- [ ] blouses, shirts, socks, underwear *(take a limited supply—use wash and wear)*
- [ ] shorts, long slacks, jeans, skirts *(take a limited supply)*
- [ ] sunglasses
- [ ] walking shoes *(plenty of walking! Good shoes are very important!)*
- [ ] swimsuit
- [ ] personal modesty kit *(for entering "holy places" and orthodox communities)*
- [ ] heavy sweater or jacket
- [ ] hat
- [ ] flip-flops, thongs, or old sneakers *(for the beach)*
- [ ] bedroom slippers and pajamas

TOILETRIES/MEDICATIONS

- [ ] shaving equipment
- [ ] eye drops or contact lens solutions and cleaners*
- [ ] athlete's foot treatment, Band-Aids
- [ ] diarrhea medicine
- [ ] cold remedy or decongestant tablets
- [ ] sleeping pills
- [ ] motion sickness pills
- [ ] nail clippers, file
- [ ] toothbrush and paste, dental floss

- ☐ deodorant
- ☐ suntan lotion, sunburn medication/ointment
- ☐ personal soap (hotel will furnish small bars)*
- ☐ comb and hairbrush
- ☐ shampoo
- ☐ aspirin or other nonprescription medications
- ☐ copies of any prescriptions (in case you need them filled)
- ☐ package of towelettes
- ☐ earplugs
- ☐ other personal hygiene products

MISCELLANEOUS

- ☐ travel alarm
- ☐ plastic bags (to wrap wet wash cloth, laundry, etc.)
- ☐ pen, notebook, and small Bible (Old and New Testament)
- ☐ small sewing kit
- ☐ adapter or converter for all electrical appliances
- ☐ tiny flashlight
- ☐ handkerchiefs or tissues
- ☐ laundry detergent (small supply)*
- ☐ washcloth
- ☐ camera, film, extra batteries
- ☐ extra pair of eyeglasses (or prescription)
- ☐ electrical appliances (hair dryer, razor, travel iron)*
- ☐ cassette recorder*
- ☐ small umbrella or rain hat (November–April)
- ☐ boxed snacks (individually packed, travel size)*

ITEMS TO PACK IN HAND LUGGAGE

- ☐ airline tickets
- ☐ passport
- ☐ one-day change of clothes
- ☐ essential toiletries
- ☐ neck pillow and sleeping mask (for sleeping on airplane)
- ☐ good book (to read on the flight over and back)

Conversational
Hebrew and Arabic

English is widely spoken throughout the land of Israel, but sometime you might enjoy trying to converse with someone using his or her native tongue. Following are a few useful Hebrew and Arabic phrases you can master to feel more "at home" in Israel.

ENGLISH	HEBREW	ARABIC
Hello	*Shalom*	*Marhaba*
Good-bye	*Shalom*	*Salaam Aleichem*
Thank you	*Todah Rabah*	*Shookran*
Good morning	*Boker Tov*	*Sabah Al-Khayr*
Good evening	*Erev Tov*	*Massa Al-Khayr*
Yes	*Ken*	*Na'am*
No	*Lo*	*La*
Do you speak English?	*ah-TAH m'dah-BEHR Bit-kal-LAM angLEET?*	*inGLEEZI?*
How much (does it cost)?	*KA-mah?*	*ah-DESH hadah?*
Where is . . ?	*AY-fo?*	*Wen?*
Water	*Mayim*	*Mayya*
Jerusalem	*Yerushalayim*	*al-Quds*
Pardon/Excuse me	*slee-CHA*	*sa-MECH-nee*
Taxi	*shay-ROOT*	*shay-ROOT*
The land of Israel	*Eretz Yisrael*	*Palestine*

How to Overcome Jet Lag

Rapid travel through multiple time zones can take its toll on the traveler's physical and mental well-being. "Jet lag" is the phrase used to describe the condition when an individual's internal body clock is out of sync with the actual time in the region to which he or she has traveled. The clock on the wall says that it is the middle of the night, but the traveler's body awakens and refuses to go back to sleep. Jet lag can result in lethargy, sleeplessness, constipation or diarrhea, and illness. At the very least it can make a person feel "out of sorts" for the first two or three days of the trip.

Several simple techniques have been developed to help an individual overcome the symptoms of jet lag and adjust his or her internal body clock to the new time zone as rapidly as possible. These principles are used by government employees who travel around the world and who must operate at peak efficiency the minute they arrive. The principles are explained fully in the book, *Overcoming Jet Lag* by Charles F. Ehret and Lynne Waller Scanlon. The following information is loosely adapted from the book and applied specifically to flights to Israel. If you follow these principles, you will find that your body will adjust very rapidly to the change in time zones. This will make your trip more enjoyable.

The time difference between the eastern United States and Israel is seven hours. That is, when it is noon in New York City, it is 7:00 P.M. in Jerusalem. The following instructions will help you overcome jet lag on your way to Israel. It is sometimes difficult to follow these principles exactly, but the more you are able to follow them, the easier you will find it to adjust your internal body clock.

THE DAY OF THE FLIGHT

1. Get out of bed earlier than usual.

2. Eat a high protein breakfast and lunch, and a high carbohydrate supper.

3. Drink a lot of water or decaffeinated beverages to compensate for the dehydration that is common on long airline flights.

4. Shortly after the evening meal on your transatlantic flight, set your wristwatch ahead to your destination time.

5. Since it is now early morning destination time, try to rest or sleep as soon as possible. Pull down your window shade, put on a sleeping mask, or take a sleeping aid—but go to sleep!

BREAKFAST, DESTINATION TIME

1. Do not oversleep. Walk around to activate your body and brain.

2. Drink one to two cups of black coffee, strong tea, or caffeinated soft drinks between 6:00 and 8:00 A.M. destination time or when breakfast is served on the airplane.

3. Keep active all day, and do not nap! Go to bed by 10:00 P.M. destination time. You might want to take a sleeping aid to make sure you go to sleep immediately.

4. If you wake up in the middle of the night, try to go back to sleep.

FIRST TOURING DAY

Your body should be almost adjusted to the change in time zones. Eat well, keep active, don't allow yourself to nap, and enjoy your time in Israel. Take a sleeping aid for one last night.

Requirements for Obtaining a U.S. Passport

1. Obtain a passport application from your district or county clerk's office, the post office, or your local travel agency. (The county clerk's office is usually at the county courthouse.)

2. Fill out the application and take it back to the district clerk with the following additional items:

    - A certified birth certificate with state, city, or county seal. Hospital birth certificates or "notification of birth" certificates are not acceptable. You must present a certified birth certificate.
    - Two identical, recently made two-by-two inch photos with image size between one and three-eights inches from bottom of chin to top of hair with plain white background. Photos must be clear, front view, full face, and taken in normal street attire (no hats or dark glasses). These photos can be obtained at most camera shops and photography studios with no wait and at a reasonable price.
    - A valid driver's license, a military I.D., or a state-issued picture I.D.
    - A check or money order for the cost of the passport payable to "Department of State." (They will not accept cash for this amount.) In addition, you should bring some cash for the processing fee that your county office may charge. (Some offices may not accept a check for this portion.)
    - Your Social Security number.

- Applicants thirteen years of age and over must appear in person at the district clerk's office. Applications for minors under the age of thirteen must be done in person by a natural parent who is named on the birth certificate.
- Certified proof of name change (required only if your name is different than that appearing on your birth certificate), such as a marriage license.

3. The above information applies to all new passport applications for individuals eighteen years of age and older. Following are some exceptions for those renewing their passports and for those under eighteen years of age:

    - To renew your passport, you only need to obtain an application for passport renewal from the district clerk, the post office, or your local travel agency. You can mail the application (along with your old or expired passport) directly to the passport office listed on the form (with, of course, a check for the cost of the passport).
    - The fee to "Department of State" for applicants seventeen years of age or younger is less than the amount of a passport for an adult.

4. Keep your receipt until your passport and submitted documents have been returned to you.

5. If you already have a valid passport but have changed your name, you must get your passport changed. This is done without charge. Forms to update your passport can be obtained from the district clerk, the post office, or your local travel agency.

6. Passports remain valid for ten years when obtained at eighteen years of age and older; five years when obtained under eighteen.

A Four-Week Schedule of Bible Reading and Prayer to Prepare for Israel

	Specific Bible Readings	Specific Items for Prayer
Week #1:	Focus on the land	Pray for the group
Day 1	Deuteronomy 8:6–20	Safety of the group
Day 2	Deuteronomy 11:8–21	Physical health and strength of the group
Day 3	Psalm 42	Unity and harmony of the group
Day 4	Psalm 121	Spirit of excitement among the group
Day 5	Proverbs 24:30–34	Joyful attitude among the group
Day 6	Isaiah 40:1–11	Smooth travel arrangements for the group
Day 7	Luke 8:4–15	The forging of new friendships within the group
Week #2:	Focus on Galilee	Pray for those who assist the tour
Day 1	Isaiah 9:1–7	The guide
Day 2	Luke 4:14–30	The bus driver
Day 3	Matthew 4:18–5:12	The tour host or pastor
Day 4	John 2:1–11	The travel agent and land operator

Day 5	Matthew 8:5–17	The airline pilots and flight attendants
Day 6	Mark 5:35–43	The airport baggage handlers
Day 7	Matthew 16:13–28	The hotel staff

Week #3:	Focus on the hill country	Pray for yourself
Day 1	Joshua 10:1–15	Ability to retain information
Day 2	Joshua 24:1–15	Spiritual discernment
Day 3	1 Samuel 17:1–50	Adaptability and flexibility
Day 4	1 Kings 18:16–46	A quiet witness to those you meet
Day 5	2 Kings 17:5–23	Physical strength and stamina
Day 6	Nehemiah 4:1–15	Personal safety
Day 7	John 4:1–42	A Christlike attitude

Week #4:	Focus on Jerusalem	Pray for the physical arrangements
Day 1	Psalm 122	Good weather
Day 2	Psalm 125	Comfort on the airline flights
Day 3	Matthew 21:1–17	Safe road conditions
Day 4	Mark 14:12–52	Quiet, comfortable hotels
Day 5	Luke 24:1–53	Reliable buses
Day 6	Acts 2:1–47	Careful handling of all luggage
Day 7	Zechariah 14:1–9	Smooth travel connections

A Four-Week Bible Series to Prepare a Group Spiritually for a Trip to Israel

Week #1

Trust and Obey
DEUTERONOMY 11:1–32
God's Testing Ground of Faith

I. God's Expectations (11:1–12)

    A. God expects us to love and obey Him because of what He has done for us in the past *(11:1–7)*

        NOTE: God rehearses Israel's history from their bondage in Egypt, through their deliverance at the Red Sea . . . to their judgment in the wilderness.

    B. God expects us to love and obey Him because of His promises to us for the future *(11:8–12)*

        NOTE: God describes the Promised Land to a nation that has not yet experienced it.

        1. It's a land of promised blessing *(v. 9)*

        2. It's a land unlike anything experienced before *(v. 10)*

        3. It's a land under God's care *(vv. 11–12)*

II. God's Response (11:13–21)

A. God will bless those who trust and obey *(11:13–15)*

1. God will provide the needed rain *(vv. 13–14a)*

NOTE: Israel's rainy season extends from late November to early March, but in a good year the rains begin in October and extend into April. The "early rain and the latter rain" are these extensions and signal abundant rainfall and a good harvest.

2. God will provide the needed food for the people and their animals *(vv. 14b–15)*

NOTE: The "grain" refers to wheat and barley, Israel's main food source. The "wine" comes from the vineyards, and the "oil" from the olive tree. These are four of the seven main species of the land that God promised Israel *(see Deut. 8:7–8).*

B. God will judge those who turn from Him *(11:16–21)*

1. God's warning against turning from Him *(vv. 16–17)*

2. God's remedy for turning from Him *(vv. 18–21)*

a. Know His Word *(v. 18)*

NOTE: Orthodox Jews today take this literally and bind phylacteries on their arms and foreheads when praying.

b. Teach His Word *(v. 19)*

c. Exalt His Word in the home and in the city *(vv. 20–21)*

NOTE: Orthodox Jews today take this literally and place mezuzahs (a box containing a portion of God's Word) on the door frames of their homes and businesses and on the gates of the city of Jerusalem.

III. God's Reminder (11:22–32)

A. God reminded the people of His promises before they entered the land *(11:22–25)*

    1. Obedience brings victory over opposition *(vv. 22–23)*

    2. Obedience brings victory over limitations *(v. 24)*

    3. Obedience brings victory over obstacles *(v. 25)*

B. God commanded the people to remember His promises after they entered the land *(11:26–32)*

> NOTE: Israel fulfilled this command in Joshua 8:30–35. Mount Ebal and Mount Gerizim today stand guard over the Arab city of Nablus.

Conclusion: The land of Israel was God's "testing ground of faith." God expected His children to move ahead by faith and take the land He had promised them. But their walk of faith was not to end once the land had been conquered. God wants His followers to live out His command to "trust and obey."

NOTE: Conclude with the hymn, "Trust and Obey."

Week #2

It Is Well with My Soul

ISAIAH 40:1–31

Comfort in Times of Discouragement

I. **The Announcement of Comfort (40:1–5)**

A. The announcement from God in heaven *(40:1–2)*

NOTE: The three promises of God foreshadow the three main themes of Isaiah 40–66.

1. "Her warfare is accomplished" looks to Israel's deliverance from Babylon *(Isa. 40–48)*

2. "Her iniquity is pardoned" looks to Israel's redemption from sin *(Isa. 49–57)*

3. "She has received . . . double" looks to Israel's double portion of blessing in the future *(Isa. 58–66)* *[For this use of "double" see Isa. 61:7.]*

B. The announcement from a voice in the wilderness *(40:3–5)*

NOTE: The "wilderness" being described is the Judean wilderness that lies between Jerusalem and Jericho and along the western edge of the Dead Sea. Verse 4 is a perfect picture of this land and offers hope by showing that God can "change the unchangeable."

1. The call to preparation *(v. 3)*

2. The removal of all obstacles *(v. 4)*

3. The appearance of God's glory *(v. 5)*

II. The Reasons for Comfort (40:6–26)

A. The certainty of God's Word *(40:6–8)*

1. People are temporal *(vv. 6–8a)*

   NOTE: Isaiah described the grass and flowers that grow in the Judean wilderness during the winter rainy season. Once the rains end and the hot east wind blows in from the Arabian desert, the grass and flowers wither and die.

2. God's Word stands forever *(v. 8b)*

   NOTE: People, problems, and circumstances come and go just like the wildflowers in the Judean wilderness. But we can find hope in God's Word of promise that will never fail.

B. The surety of God's character *(40:9–26)*

1. God's power and love are constant *(vv. 9–11)*

   NOTE: Isaiah challenged the people to look closely at the character of the God offering them comfort and deliverance.

   a. God has the might of a conquering hero *(vv. 9–10)*

   b. God has the compassion of a tender shepherd *(v. 11)*

2. God's strength is mightier than any opposition *(vv. 12–26)*

   NOTE: Isaiah asks, and answers, a series of questions to show that God is superior to any possible opposition we might face. Our God is bigger than our problems!

   a. God is superior to nations *(vv. 12–17)*

      (1) The questions *(vv. 12–14)*

      (2) The application to God *(vv. 15–17)*

   b. God is superior to idols *(vv. 18–20)*

      (1). The questions *(v. 18)*

      (2). The application to God *(vv. 19–20)*

    c.   God is superior to human leaders *(vv. 21–24)*

        (1) The questions *(v. 21)*

        (2). The application to God (vv. 22–24)

    d.   God is superior to all cosmic forces *(vv. 25–26)*

        (1) The questions *(v. 25)*

        (2) The application to God *(v. 26)*

III. The Requirements for Receiving Comfort (40:27–31)

    A. Remember God's goodness *(40:27–28)*

       1. The complaint: God doesn't know or care for me *(v. 27)*

       2. The solution: Realize God's awesome character and power *(v. 28)*

           a.   God made all

           b.   God sustains all

           c.   God understands all

    B. Wait on God to solve your problems *(40:29–31)*

       1. Human strength will fail *(vv. 29–30)*

       2. Those who depend on God's strength will succeed *(v. 31)*

Conclusion: The Judean wilderness served as an object lesson to the nation of Israel. It stood as an obstacle between Jerusalem and Jericho—harsh, foreboding, and unchangeable. It symbolized their problems that often seemed overwhelming, unsolvable, and utterly discouraging. God's reminder in times of trouble is to focus on Him, not on our problems. He is mightier than our problems and stronger than our opposition. And He desires to bear us up on wings of eagles. The God who can change the craggy wilderness into a smooth plain is the God who can cause us to say—even as we face our trials—"It is well with my soul!"

NOTE: Conclude with the hymn, "It Is Well with My Soul."

Week #3

A Great Prophet in Our Midst!

2 KINGS 4:8–37; LUKE 7:11–17

The Ministries of Elisha and Jesus

I. Elisha's Ministry in Shunem (2 Kings 4:8–37)

A. The birth of a child *(4:8–17)*

> NOTE: The village of Shunem rests on the southern slopes of the hill of Moreh. Prior to the time of Elisha, this city had known terror . . . and honor. The Philistines captured the village and used it as their base when they gathered to fight against Saul and the Israelites *(1 Sam. 28:4)*. Later a woman from Shunem named Abishag was chosen to take care of King David in his old age *(1 Kings 1:3–4)*.

1. The woman's kindness to Elisha *(4:8–10)*

2. Elisha's kindness to the woman *(4:11–17)*

> NOTE: In the Old Testament, barrenness was a sign of cursing. The woman displayed faith in recognizing Elisha as prophet, and she displayed compassion in providing for his needs. God blessed her with fruitfulness for her kindness.

B. The "second birth" of the child *(4:18–37)*

> NOTE: After the miraculous birth of the child, one expected the family to live "happily ever after." The sudden death of the child was a severe test of the woman's faith, but her quick, decisive response revealed her depth of trust.

1. The child's death *(vv. 18–21)*

> NOTE: The child went out to his father who was "with the reapers." This would place the event in the spring during wheat or barley harvest. The sun can become brutally hot in the late morning, and the cooling breeze from the Mediterranean Sea doesn't usually arrive until the early afternoon. The child may have been overcome by the intense morning sun because he died at noon *(v. 20)*.

2. The woman's journey to Elisha *(vv. 22–30)*

> NOTE: The woman rode across the Jezreel Valley from Shunem to Mount Carmel in the heat of the day to summon Elisha.

3. Elisha's miracle of restoring the boy to life *(vv. 31–37)*

> NOTE: After raising the boy, Elisha gave him back to his mother. "Then she took her son and went out" *(v. 37)*.

The scene now shifts forward in time nine hundred years to another small town on the hill of Moreh.

II. Jesus' Ministry in Nain (Luke 7:11–17)

A. Jesus' arrival in the village *(7:11–13)*

> NOTE: The village of Nain rests on the northern slopes of the hill of Moreh, approximately two miles from Shunem. The parallels to Elisha's miracle in the area are obvious . . . and intentional.

1. The event takes place on the slopes of the hill of Moreh

2. The dead child is an only son

3. The account focuses on the response of the mother

4. Each account focuses on a man of God recognized as a prophet

B. Jesus' raising of the widow's son *(7:14–15)*

1. Jesus restored the boy to life *(v. 14)*

2. Jesus gave the child back to his mother *(v. 15)*

> NOTE: Jesus' actions paralleled those of Elisha. Elisha summoned the Shunammite woman and commanded her to "take your son." Jesus gave the boy "back to his mother."

C. The crowd's response to the miracle *(7:16–17)*

> **NOTE:** The crowd understood the significance of Jesus' miracle when they shouted, "A great prophet has appeared among us." No doubt they saw the connection between Jesus' miracle and the one performed by Elisha on the same mountain nearly nine hundred years earlier.

Conclusion: Much of Jesus' ministry focused on visibly reminding the people of Israel that the God who had delivered them in the past was now at work in their midst. The miracles validated His claims to be God's Son, Israel's Messiah, and "the Prophet" promised by Moses. This particular story gives us a glimpse into God's compassion for those who are hurting. Just as Jesus' "heart went out to her" in her time of grief, so today Peter admonishes us to "cast all your anxiety on him because he cares for you" (1 Pet. 5:7).

NOTE: Conclude with the hymn, "Day by Day."

Week #4

Lead Me to Calvary
MATTHEW 26:57–28:10

The Events of the Crucifixion

I. The Cross (26:57–27:56)

A. The trials *(26:57–27:26)*

1. The trial before the Sanhedrin *(26:57–75)*

   NOTE: Peter denied Jesus during the time Jesus was appearing before the Jewish leaders in the high priest's house. Peter had followed at a distance, but when confronted, he denied his Lord.

2. The trial before Pilate *(27:11–26)*

   NOTE: Although the exact location is uncertain, tradition says that Jesus appeared before Pilate in the Fortress of Antonia that looked over the northwestern edge of the temple. From here Jesus began His walk to "The Place of the Skull."

B. The torture *(27:27–31)*

NOTE: The Romans flogged Jesus *(v. 26)*, a lashing so severe that prisoners sometimes died from this punishment before being crucified. Jesus was then stripped, mocked, spat on, and beaten on the head with a staff. All this was "preparation" for the actual crucifixion.

C. The crucifixion *(27:32–56)*

1. Jesus' journey to Golgotha *(27:32–44)*

   NOTE: Jesus likely carried a beam of the cross until, weakened by the flogging, He collapsed. The Romans forced a Jewish passerby to carry the beam the remainder of the way. From the cross Jesus could look out at soldiers gambling for His clothes, religious leaders mocking His death, and thieves sharing His dreaded fate.

2. Jesus' death on the cross *(27:45–56)*

> NOTE: Crucifixion was a lengthy, torturous death. And yet, after paying for humanity's sin, Jesus "gave up his spirit." He did not die from the crucifixion. As He had said earlier, "I lay down my life—only to take it up again. No one takes it from me, but I lay it down of my own accord. I have authority to lay it down and authority to take it up again" *(John 10:17–18)*.

II. The Grave (27:57–66)

A. The burial at the tomb *(27:57–61)*

1. Joseph of Arimathea boldly requested the body of Jesus *(vv. 57–58)*

2. Joseph placed Jesus' body in his own new tomb *(vv. 59–61)*

> NOTE: In a "coincidence" prepared by God, Joseph's new tomb had been dug in the same area where Jesus was crucified. According to John's Gospel, "At the place where Jesus was crucified, there was a garden, and in the garden a new tomb, in which no one had ever been laid" *(John 19:41)*.

B. The guarding of the tomb *(27:62–66)*

1. The request came from the religious leaders who remembered Jesus' words *(vv. 62–64)*

2. The order came from Pilate and was carried out by his soldiers *(vv. 65–66)*

> NOTE: The belief that the disciples stole Jesus' body contradicts this key fact: Jesus' tomb was sealed and under Roman guard. The frightened disciples would have been no match for experienced soldiers. In effect, God put the tomb under protective custody to validate the truth of the Resurrection.

III. The Empty Tomb (28:1–10)

A. The opening of the tomb *(28:1–4)*

B. The announcement to the women *(28:5–10)*

1. Jesus is risen

2. The tomb is empty

3. You will see Him

Conclusion: God's "good news" for us is that Jesus died for our sins according to the Scriptures. His death was validated by His burial. He was raised on the third day according to the Scriptures. His resurrection was validated by His appearances to His disciples. Paul said this was the "good news" that he preached and by which we are saved (1 Cor. 15:1–8). During your visit to Jerusalem, you will walk the Via Dolorosa, stand at Calvary, and gaze into the empty tomb. And as you do, remember that Jesus suffered, died, and rose again . . . for you.

NOTE: Conclude with the hymn, "When I Survey the Wondrous Cross."

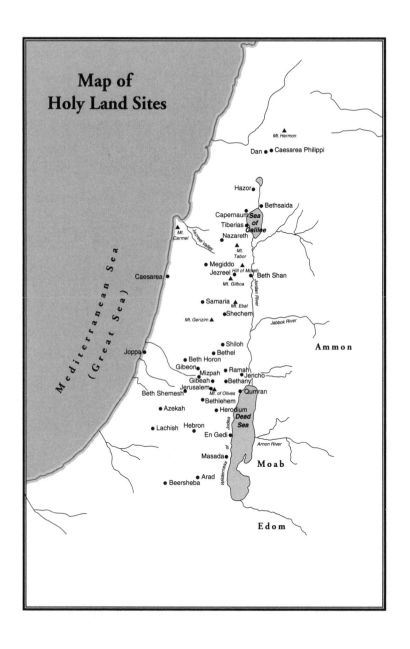

Map of
Holy Land Sites

Mt. Hermon

Dan ● ● Caesarea Philippi

Hazor ●

● Bethsaida

Capernaum ● Sea
Tiberias ● of
Nazareth Galilee

Mt.
Carmel ▲

Jezreel Valley

Mt.
Tabor ▲

Megiddo ● Hill of Moreh
Jezreel ▲ ● Beth Shan
Mt. Gilboa ▲

Jordan River

Caesarea ●

● Samaria ▲ Mt. Ebal
● Shechem

Mt. Gerizim ▲

Jabbok River

Ammon

● Shiloh
● Bethel
● Beth Horon
Gibeon ●
Mizpah ● ● Ramah
Gibeah ● ● Jericho
Jerusalem ● ● Bethany
Beth Shemesh ● Mt. of Olives ▲ ● Qumran
● Bethlehem
● Azekah ● Heronium

Joppa ●

Mediterranean Sea
(Great Sea)

Dead
Sea

● Lachish Hebron
● En Gedi

Wilderness of Judea

Arnon River

Masada ●

Moab

● Arad
● Beersheba

Edom

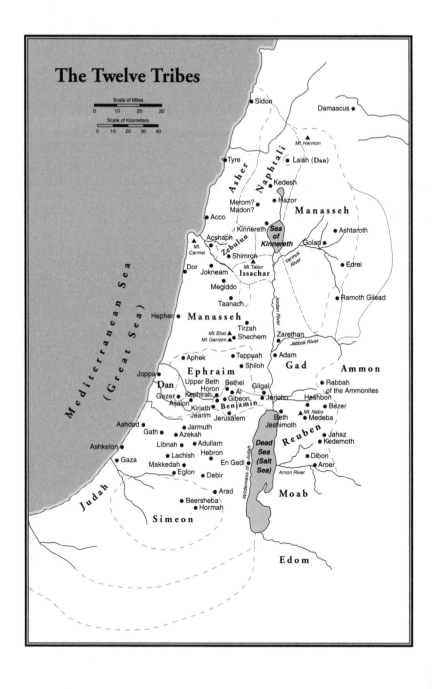

The Twelve Tribes

Scale of Miles
0 10 20 30

Scale of Kilometers
0 10 20 30 40

Mediterranean Sea (Great Sea)

Sidon

Damascus

Tyre

Mt. Hermon

Laish (Dan)

Asher

Naphtali

Kedesh

Merom?
Madon?

Hazor

Manasseh

Acco

Ashtaroth

Acshaph

Kinnereth

Sea of Kinnereth

Golan

Mt. Carmel

Zebulun

Shimron

Yarmuk River

Edrei

Dor

Jokneam

Issachar

Mt. Tabor

Megiddo

Taanach

Jordan River

Ramoth Gilead

Hepher

Manasseh

Tirzah

Mt. Ebal
Mt. Gerizim

Shechem

Zarethan

Jabbok River

Aphek

Tappuah

Adam

Shiloh

Gad

Ammon

Joppa

Ephraim

Upper Beth Horon

Bethel

Ai

Gilgal

Rabbah
of the Ammonites

Dan

Gezer

Kephirah

Gibeon

Jericho

Heshbon

Aijalon

Benjamin

Kiriath Jearim

Bezer

Mt. Nebo

Ashdod

Jerusalem

Beth Jeshimoth

Medeba

Gath

Jarmuth

Reuben

Azekah

Jahaz

Kedemoth

Ashkelon

Libnah

Adullam

Hebron

Dead Sea (Salt Sea)

Dibon

Gaza

Lachish

En Gedi

Aroer

Makkedah

Eglon

Debir

Arnon River

Arad

Moab

Wilderness of Judah

Beersheba

Hormah

Judah

Simeon

Edom

THE 12 TRIBES OF ISRAEL

The 12 tribes of Israel descended from the 12 sons of the patriarch Jacob, whom God later renamed Israel. The land assignment and relative importance of each tribe reflected the birth order, birth mother, and individual actions of each son.

RECORD OF THE SONS' BIRTHS:

Genesis 29:31–30:24; 35:16-20

KEY HISTORICAL INCIDENTS IN THE SONS' LIVES:

Genesis 34:25-31:	Simeon and Levi kill the men of Shechem
Genesis 35:21-22:	Reuben slept with his father's concubine
Genesis 37:2-11:	Joseph is hated by his brothers but the favorite of his father
Genesis 48:1-20:	Jacob blesses Joseph's two children, Ephraim and Manasseh, and "adopts" them as his own
Genesis 49:1-28:	Jacob gives a prophetic blessing to each of his sons

TRIBAL ALLOTMENTS IN THE LAND OF ISRAEL:

Numbers 32:1-42	Allotment for Reuben, Gad, and one-half of Manasseh
Joshua 15:1-63	Allotment for Judah
Joshua 16:1–17:18	Allotment for Ephraim and one-half of Manasseh
Joshua 18:11-28	Allotment for Benjamin
Joshua 19:1-9	Allotment for Simeon
Joshua 19:10-16	Allotment for Zebulun
Joshua 19:17-23	Allotment for Issachar
Joshua 19:24-31	Allotment for Asher
Joshua 19:32-39	Allotment for Naphtali
Joshua 19:40-48	Allotment for Dan
Joshua 21:1-42	Allotment for Levi

The Herods of the Bible

Herod the Great
37–4 B.C.
- King of Judea, Galilee, Iturea, and Traconitis
- Built Caesarea, the Temple, Masada, and the Herodium
- Killed the babies of Bethlehem (Matt. 2:1–18)

Herod Philip ll
4 B.C.–A.D. 34
- Tetrarch of Iturea and Traconitis (Luke 3:1)
- Built Caesarea Philippi

Archelaus
4 B.C.–A.D. 6
- Governor of Judea, Idumea, and Samaria
- Reason Joseph and Mary settled in Nazareth (Matt. 2:19–23)
- Deposed by Romans

Herod Antipas
4 B.C.–A.D. 39
- Tetrarch of Galilee and Perea (Luke 3:1)
- Built the city of Tiberias
- Married his brother's wife (Mark 6:17–18)
- Put John the Baptist to death (Matt. 14:1-12)
- Sent Jesus back to Pilate (Luke 23:5-12)

Aristobulus
- Killed by his father Herod the Great

Herod Agrippa l
A.D. 37–44
- King of Judea
- Killed James the brother of John and imprisoned Peter (Acts 12:1–19a)
- Struck down by God at Caesarea (Acts 12:19b-24)

Key to Titles

 = King

 = Tetrarch

 = Governor

Herod Agrippa ll
A.D. 44–70
- King of Judea
- Heard Paul's defense at Caesarea (Acts 25:13–26:32)
- Sided with Rome in the Jewish Revolt

THE HISTORY OF ISRAEL

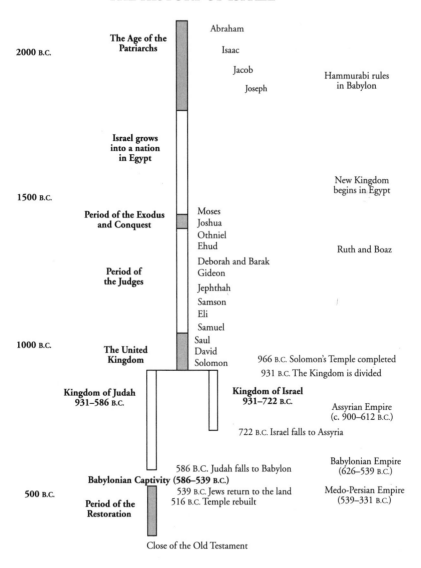

2000 B.C.

The Age of the
Patriarchs

Abraham

Isaac

Jacob

Joseph

Hammurabi rules
in Babylon

Israel grows
into a nation
in Egypt

New Kingdom
begins in Egypt

1500 B.C.

Period of the Exodus
and Conquest

Moses
Joshua
Othniel
Ehud

Ruth and Boaz

Period of
the Judges

Deborah and Barak
Gideon
Jephthah
Samson
Eli
Samuel

1000 B.C.

The United
Kingdom

Saul
David
Solomon

966 B.C. Solomon's Temple completed

931 B.C. The Kingdom is divided

Kingdom of Judah
931–586 B.C.

Kingdom of Israel
931–722 B.C.

Assyrian Empire
(c. 900–612 B.C.)

722 B.C. Israel falls to Assyria

586 B.C. Judah falls to Babylon

Babylonian Empire
(626–539 B.C.)

Babylonian Captivity (586–539 B.C.)

500 B.C.

Period of the
Restoration

539 B.C. Jews return to the land
516 B.C. Temple rebuilt

Medo-Persian Empire
(539–331 B.C.)

Close of the Old Testament

Section Two

The Land of Israel

OUTLINE OF BIBLE HISTORY

The following chart contains a summary of the historical periods that relate to biblical events in the land of Israel. This chart will help you put the different locations you will visit in their proper historical setting. The periods are as follows:

Biblical Period	Dates	Archaeological Period
Patriarchal Period	ca. 2000 B.C. to 1446 B.C.	Middle Bronze Age
Period of the Exodus	1446 B.C. to 1400 B.C.	Late Bronze Age
Period of Conquest	1400 B.C. to 1390 B.C.	
Period of the Judges	1390 B.C. to 1050 B.C.	Late Bronze/Early Iron Age
United Kingdom	1050 B.C. to 931 B.C.	Iron Age
Divided Kingdom	931 B.C. to 722 B.C.	
Single Kingdom	722 B.C. to 586 B.C.	
Babylonian Captivity	586 B.C. to 539 B.C.	
Restoration	539 B.C. to ca. 400 B.C.	Persian Period
Intertestamental Era	ca. 400 B.C. to 4 B.C.	Persian/Hellenistic Period
Life of Christ	4 B.C. to A.D. 33	Roman Period
Apostolic Age	A.D. 33 to ca. A.D. 70	

For each site in Israel listed in this book, you will find the main Scripture passages describing events that took place there. These passages are separated into their appropriate historical periods. The sites are listed alphabetically.

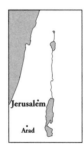

Arad

(uh RAHD) The city of Arad, located in the eastern Negev basin, controlled the road from the hill country of Judah to Edom. A large city, with extensive fortifications, dominated the site in the Early Bronze Age. A smaller Iron Age fortress guarded the road and region at the end of the Judean monarchy. One of the most remarkable discoveries at the site was a complete temple patterned after God's temple in Jerusalem.

Period of the Exodus   The king of Arad attacked the Israelites near the end of their time in the wilderness. Israel defeated the invaders and destroyed their cities, renaming the region Hormah ("destruction").
See Numbers 21:1–3

Period of Conquest   The descendants of Moses' father-in-law, the Kenites, moved from Jericho to Arad and settled in the territory of Judah.
See Judges 1:16

Reconstruction of the stone altar at Arad.

Azekah

(uh ZAKE ah) The city of Azekah guarded the western edge of the Elah Valley. Strategically located on a high hill, the city stood on the border between Israel and the Philistines.

Period of Conquest
When Joshua attacked the Canaanite kings who threatened Gibeon, he pursued them "all the way to Azekah."
See Joshua 10:10–11

God allotted Azekah to the tribe of Judah.
See Joshua 15:35

United Kingdom
When David fought Goliath, the battle took place in the Elah Valley. The Philistines camped on the southern side of the valley "between Socoh and Azekah."
See 1 Samuel 17:1

Divided Kingdom
King Rehoboam of Judah fortified Azekah as one of his cities of defense.
See 2 Chronicles 11:9

Single Kingdom
Nebuchadnezzar, king of Babylon, invaded Judah and sent his army against Judah's cities. Near the end of his invasion, only Lachish, Azekah, and Jerusalem remained unconquered. Eventually they all fell.
See Jeremiah 34:7

Restoration
Some of the remnant who returned from captivity in Babylon reinhabited Azekah.
See Nehemiah 11:30

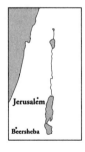

Jerusalem

Beersheba

Beersheba

(behr SHEB ah, "well of the oath" or "well of the seven") The city of Beersheba was, practically speaking, the southernmost city of Israel in the Old Testament. When the writers of Scripture wanted to speak of all Israel (from north to south), they would say "from Dan to Beersheba" (cf. Judg. 20:1; 1 Sam. 3:20; 2 Sam. 3:10; 17:11; 24:2, 15; 1 Kings 4:25). Beersheba controlled the central Negev basin.

Patriarchal Period	When Hagar and Ishmael were forced to leave Abraham's camp, they wandered in the wilderness of Beersheba. *See Genesis 21:14*
	Abraham made an agreement, paid seven ewe lambs, and took an oath with Abimelech to establish ownership over a well Abraham had dug. The place was named Beersheba ("well of the oath" or "well of the seven"). *See Genesis 21:25–34*
	Isaac also quarreled with Abimelech and took an oath. That same day his servants found water, and Isaac named the place Beersheba ("well of the oath"). *See Genesis 26:26–33*
Patriarchal Period	Jacob stole the birthright from Esau while the family camped at Beersheba. He then left Beersheba and traveled to Haran to find a wife. *See Genesis 28:10.*

Jacob paused at Beersheba to offer sacrifices before leaving the Promised Land for Egypt. *See Genesis 46:1–7*

Period of Conquest

Beersheba was located in the territory given to the tribe of Judah. But God allotted the city to the tribe of Simeon, who had their inheritance scattered among the tribe of Judah.
See Joshua 15:28; 19:2

Samuel's sons judged Israel in Beersheba. *See 1 Samuel 8:1–2*

Divided Kingdom

Elijah stopped at Beersheba as he fled from Jezebel. He left his servant there, but he continued to flee south for another day.
See 1 Kings 19:1–4

Single Kingdom

Under King Josiah's reforms, the high place inside the city of Beersheba was torn down. *See 2 Kings 23:8*

Restoration

Some of the remnant who returned from captivity in Babylon reinhabited Beersheba. *See Nehemiah 11:27*

Well of Beersheba.

Beth Horon
Jerusalem

Beth Horon

(beth HOH rahn, "house of caves") Two villages, Upper Beth Horon and Lower Beth Horon, straddled the ridge that extends from the Aijalon Valley to the hill country just north of Jerusalem. These towns guarded the main road from the Mediterranean coast to Jerusalem.

Period of Conquest

Joshua chased the Canaanites along the "road down from Beth Horon to Azekah" when he rescued Gibeon.
See Joshua 10:9–14

Beth Horon was on the border between the tribes of Benjamin and Ephraim.
See Joshua 16:1–5; 18:13–14

God allotted Beth Horon to the Levites as one of their forty-eight cities of inheritance throughout the land of Israel.
See Joshua 21:20–22

United Kingdom

The Philistines sent raiding parties along the road at Beth Horon when they threatened Israel in the days of King Saul.
See 1 Samuel 13:17–18

Solomon fortified Beth Horon to protect the main road to Jerusalem.
See 1 Kings 9:17; 2 Chronicles 8:5

Divided Kingdom

Troops of Amaziah, king of Judah, rioted and raided cities of Judah from Beth Horon to Samaria when they were sent home from battle.
See 2 Chronicles 25:13

Beth Shan/Scythopolis

(beth SHAHN, "house of security"; *sih THAHP oh liss,* "city of the Scythians")*Beth Shan is located at the strategic juncture of the Jezreel and Jordan Valleys. Like Jericho, Beth Shan was almost continuously occupied throughout history. During the intertestamental period, the city was renamed Scythopolis. Today archaeologists are uncovering the extensive ruins of Roman/Byzantine Scythopolis.

Period of Conquest

God allotted Beth Shan to the tribe of Manasseh, but they were unable to drive out the Canaanites because "all the Canaanites who live in the plain have iron chariots, both those in Beth Shan and its settlements and those in the Valley of Jezreel" (Josh. 17:16). *See Joshua 17:11, 16; Judges 1:27*

United Kingdom

After defeating Saul and his sons on Mount Gilboa, the Philistines hanged their bodies on the walls of Beth Shan.

See 1 Samuel 31:10–12

Solomon placed Beth Shan, Megiddo, and Jezreel under the governorship of Baana, son of Ahilud.
See 1 Kings 4:12

Tel-Beth Shan, the site of the Old Testament city.

Life of Christ Scythopolis was one of the chief cities of the Decapolis—a league of ten cities sharing Greek culture and government.

Beth
Shemesh
Jerusalem

Beth Shemesh

(beth SHEM mesh, "house of the sun") Beth Shemesh sits at the eastern end of the Sorek Valley. This city, assigned to the Levites, marked the historical border between Israel and the Philistines.

Period of Conquest

Beth Shemesh was on the border between the tribes of Judah and Dan.
See Joshua 15:10

God allotted Beth Shemesh to the Levites as one of their forty-eight cities of inheritance throughout the land of Israel.
See Joshua 21:16

Period of the Judges

Samson was a Danite who lived in the Sorek Valley near Beth Shemesh. Zorah, Eshtaol, and Timnah are all near Beth Shemesh.
See Judges 13–16

When the Philistines returned the ark of the covenant to the Israelites, it went by cart to Beth Shemesh. Some Israelites were killed when they looked inside the ark, so the people of Beth Shemesh refused to let the ark stay in their town.
See 1 Samuel 6:7–21

Divided Kingdom

King Amaziah of Judah was defeated and captured by King Jehoash of Israel at Beth Shemesh. The army of Israel then went to Jerusalem and tore down sections of the wall.
See 2 Kings 14:11–14; 2 Chronicles 25:21–24

The Philistines captured Beth Shemesh during the reign of King Ahaz. Ahaz appealed to the Assyrians for help in recapturing this land.
See 2 Chronicles 28:16–18

Bethany

(*BETH uh nih*, "house of song," "house of afflic-tion")Bethany was a small village on the east slope of the Mount of Olives, about two miles from Jerusalem. Jesus often spent the night in Bethany during His visits to Jerusalem.

Life of Christ

Mary, Martha, and Lazarus lived in Bethany.
See John 11:1; Mark 14:3

Jesus stayed in Bethany when He visited Jerusalem. Here Mary sat at Jesus' feet while Martha was serving.
See Matthew 21:17; Mark 11:11; Luke 10:38–42

Jesus raised Lazarus from the dead in Bethany. Today the city's Arabic name is al-Azariyya, pre-serving the town's connection to Lazarus.
See John 11:1–44

In the house of Simon the leper, Mary anointed Jesus with expensive ointment.
See Matthew 26:6–13; Mark 14:3–9; John 12:1–8

Between Bethany and Bethphage, Jesus asked two of His disciples to get a donkey and a colt for His triumphal entry.
See Mark 11:1–11; Luke 19:29–40

Jesus cursed a fruitless fig tree here, and it withered.
See Matthew 21:18–22; Mark 11:12–14

Jesus ascended to heaven from the Mount of Olives near "the vicinity of Bethany."
See Luke 24:50–53

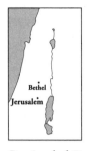

Bethel

(BETH el, "house of God") Bethel, a strategic village in the hill country of Israel, sat on the internal north/south road from Shechem to Beersheba, where that road intersected another road coming into the hill country from Jericho. Bethel played a major role in Israel's religious history.

Patriarchal Period

Abraham camped near Bethel and built an altar to the Lord.
See Genesis 12:8; 13:3

On his journey to Haran, Jacob camped at Bethel and had a vision of angels ascending and descending a stairway between earth and heaven.
See Genesis 28:10–22

Jacob returned to Bethel and built an altar to God.
See Genesis 35:1–15

Period of Conquest

The men of Bethel joined forces with the men of Ai to fight against Israel. Israel evidently captured Bethel when they defeated Ai.
See Joshua 8:10–17; 12:16

Although Bethel rested on the border between the tribes of Ephraim and Benjamin, God allotted Bethel to Benjamin.
See Joshua 16:1–2; 18:13, 22

Period of the Judges

The "house of Joseph" (Ephraim) captured Bethel and claimed it for themselves.
See Judges 1:22–26

The prophetess/judge Deborah held court between Ramah and Bethel.
See Judges 4:4–5

Period of the Judges   Samuel included Bethel on the circuit of cities from which he judged Israel.
See 1 Samuel 7:16

Divided Kingdom   Jeroboam, the first king of the northern kingdom of Israel, set up golden calves in Dan and Bethel to keep the people from going to Jerusalem to worship.
See 1 Kings 12:26–33

Jeroboam's hand was temporarily shriveled when he opposed a prophet sent by God to condemn the false worship at Bethel.
See 1 Kings 13:1–6

A group of young men from Bethel were mauled by bears when they mocked the prophet Elisha.
See 2 Kings 2:23–24

The prophets Hosea and Amos predicted the destruction of the temple of Bethel and the captivity of Israel.
See Hosea 10:15; Amos 4:4; 9:1–2

The high priest at Bethel rejected the message of Amos and brought God's judgment on his own household as a result.
See Amos 7:10–17

Single Kingdom   King Josiah of Judah destroyed the temple and defiled the altar at Bethel set up by Jeroboam.
See 2 Kings 23:15–16

Restoration   Some of the remnant who returned from captivity in Babylon reinhabited Bethel.
See Ezra 2:28; Nehemiah 7:32; 11:3

Jerusalem
Bethlehem

Bethlehem

(BETH le hem, "house of bread") Bethlehem was originally a small village just east of the main road through the hill country of Judah. The village received enough rainfall to support agriculture, but it was also close enough to the Judean wilderness to encourage the raising of sheep and goats.

Patriarchal Period

The tomb of Rachel, wife of Jacob and mother of Joseph and Benjamin, is just outside Bethlehem. Rachel died while giving birth to Benjamin.
See Genesis 35:16–20; 48:7

Period of the Judges

The story of Ruth and Boaz took place here in the spring during the barley and wheat harvest.
See the Book of Ruth

United Kingdom

David was born in Bethlehem and anointed here by Samuel as king of Israel. David was called from tending his father's flocks to shepherd the nation of Israel.
See 1 Samuel 16:1–13; 17:12

Although David was a shepherd in Bethlehem, he traveled to the Valley of Elah, where he killed Goliath.
See 1 Samuel 17:15, 34–37

While fleeing from King Saul, David longed for water from the well at Bethlehem.
See 2 Samuel 23:13–17

Divided Kingdom

Micah prophesied that the Messiah would be born in the village of Bethlehem.
See Micah 5:2

Life of Christ

In fulfillment of the prophecy of Micah 5:2, Jesus Christ was born in Bethlehem.
See Luke 2:1–7

The shepherds visited the infant Jesus in Bethlehem.
See Luke 2:8–20

The wise men, led by the star, visited and worshiped the infant "King of the Jews" in Bethlehem.
See Matthew 2:1–12

Harvesting wheat in Bethlehem.

Joseph fled with Mary and Jesus to Egypt to avoid the cruelty of Herod, who killed all the babies of Bethlehem two years old and under in a vain attempt to destroy the Lord's Messiah.
See Matthew 2:13–18

Small entrance to the Church of the Nativity in Bethlehem. Archway was filled to keep out horsemen.

Bethsaida

(beth SAY ih duh, "house of fishing") Bethsaida was a town east of the Jordan River and just north of the Sea of Galilee. Philip the Tetrarch extensively rebuilt Bethsaida and renamed it "Julias" after Julia, the daughter of Augustus Caesar.

Life of Christ

Jesus rebuked Bethsaida for refusing to repent in spite of the miracles He performed there.
See Matthew 11:20–22

Jesus healed a blind man outside Bethsaida.
See Mark 8:22–26

Jesus fed the five thousand near Bethsaida.
See Luke 9:10–17

Bethsaida was the hometown of the apostles Peter, Andrew, and Philip.
See John 1:44

Plain of Bethsaida on northeastern shore of the Sea of Galilee.

Caesarea

(*sess uh REE uh,* "pertaining to Caesar") Caesarea was originally a poor harbor on the Mediterranean coast that was called Strato's Tower. The city of Caesarea was founded by Herod the Great in 22 B.C. and was the seat of the Roman government in Palestine for over five hundred years. Herod completely rebuilt the city and named it Caesarea in honor of Augustus Caesar. Caesarea was the home of the Roman procurators, including Pontius Pilate, whose name was discovered here on an inscription that identified him as the "prefect of Judea." The existing walls and gate of the harbor were built in the time of the Crusades (twelfth century A.D.). The theater and aqueduct were built by Herod the Great and later modified by the Romans in the second century A.D.

The Mediterranean Sea as seen through the arches of the Herodian aqueduct at Caesarea.

Apostolic Age

Philip, one of the seven "deacons" in Jerusalem (Acts 6:5), was the first to preach in Caesarea. He settled there and had four daughters who prophesied.
See Acts 8:40; 21:8–9

Peter came to Caesarea in response to a vision at Joppa and preached the gospel in Cornelius's home. The Holy Spirit was poured out as at Pentecost, showing that the door of the gospel was now open to the Gentiles.
See Acts 10

Apostolic Age

God struck down Herod Agrippa I in Caesarea for accepting the worship of others who called him a god and for persecuting the early church.
See Acts 12:19–24

The turbulent waters of the Mediterranean Sea as seen from Caesarea.

Paul visited the city three times, and on the third occasion he was warned that if he went to Jerusalem he would be captured by the Jews and delivered to the Gentiles.
See Acts 9:30; 18:22; 21:8–16

Paul spent two years in prison in Caesarea. He made his defense in three outstanding addresses before Felix and Festus (Roman governors or procurators) and before King Herod Agrippa II.
See Acts 23:23–27:2

Performances are once again held at the restored Herodian theater at Caesarea.

Caesarea Philippi

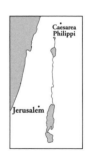

(sess uh REE uh FIL ih pie, "Caesarea of Philip")
Caesarea Philippi was originally called Panion or
Panias. Herod the Great's son, Philip, established it
as the capital of his tetrarchy and named it Caesarea
to honor the emperor. It was known as Caesarea
Philippi ("Philip's Caesarea"), to distinguish it from
other cities with the same name.

Intertestamental Era   Antiochus III of Syria defeated the
Egyptians at Panias in 197 B.C. and took
control of the region. This control by the
Seleucid dynasty set the stage for the oppres-
sion of the Jews by Antiochus IV and the
revolt of the Maccabees.

Life of Christ   Caesarea Philippi marked the northernmost
limit of Christ's ministry.
See Matthew 16:13; Mark 8:27

Peter made his confession of
Christ's deity in response to
Jesus' question: "Who do
people say the Son of Man
is?" in the region of Caesarea
Philippi.
*See Matthew 16:13–16;
Mark 8:27–30;
Luke 9:18–21*

*Stone niche at Caesarea Philippi, in
which the statue of a pagan god was
placed.*

Capernaum

(kuh PUHR nay uhm) The name Capernaum is a Greek transliteration of the Hebrew words *Kephar Nahum*—"the village of Nahum." Capernaum became a major city in the time of Christ because it was located on the Sea of Galilee (and had access to the fishing industry there) and because it straddled the International Highway, which went from Mesopotamia to Egypt, at one of its narrowest points. Thus, it controlled trade along this important highway. Its prominence is indicated by the presence of a Roman centurion and detachment of troops (Matt. 8:5–9), a customs station (Matt. 9:9), and a high officer of the king (John 4:46).

Life of Christ

Rejected at Nazareth, Jesus moved to Capernaum and made it the center of His activity for eighteen to twenty months.
See Matthew 4:13–16

Peter, Andrew, James, and John were called to be disciples near Capernaum.
See Matthew 4:18–22; Mark 1:16–21

Jesus called Matthew (Levi) from the office of the Capernaum tax or toll house to be His disciple. (Tolls were collected on the traffic from Mesopotamia and Damascus through Capernaum to the coast and Egypt.)
See Matthew 9:9–13; Mark 2:14

Jesus taught in the synagogue at Capernaum, delivered a man from an unclean spirit, and also healed Peter's mother-in-law as well as many others.
See Mark 1:21–34; Luke 4:31–41

Life of Christ

Jesus healed the centurion's servant. Capernaum was a Roman military center and this Roman centurion helped fund the construction of the Jewish synagogue in Capernaum.
See Matthew 8:5–13; Luke 7:1–10

A paralyzed man was let down through the roof and healed by Jesus in Capernaum.
See Matthew 9:1–8; Mark 2:1–12;
Luke 5:17–26

In Capernaum, Jesus raised Jairus's daughter from the dead and healed the woman who had a hemorrhage.
See Matthew 9:18–26; Mark 5:22–43;
Luke 8:40–56

Jesus also healed a nobleman's son in Capernaum.
See John 4:46–54

Two blind men and a dumb demoniac were healed in Capernaum.
See Matthew 9:27–35; 12:22–45;
Mark 3:20–22; Luke 11:14–26

Many sick people were brought to Jesus and healed in Capernaum. In fact, more of Christ's recorded miracles were performed in Capernaum than in any other city. Yet Capernaum did not believe (Matt. 11:23–24).
See Matthew 8:16–17; 9:36–38

Carmel (Mount)

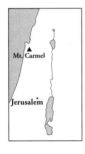

(KAHR ml, "garden of God") Mount Carmel is a wooded mountain range, somewhat triangular in shape, thirteen miles long, projecting into the Mediterranean Sea at Haifa. The mountain rises from the sea so sharply that the rapidly rising air deposits its moisture as rain or dew. Thus, the mountain is lush year-round. Only a catastrophic drought would cause Mount Carmel to turn brown and wither. From antiquity, altars to strange gods were erected on its heights and it was, particularly, a sanctuary for the worship of Baal.

United Kingdom   Solomon compared the stately majesty of his bride's head to the summit of Carmel.
See Song of Songs 7:5

Divided Kingdom   Elijah had his contest with the prophets of Baal on Mount Carmel.
See 1 Kings 18:19–39

Elijah killed the prophets of Baal at the foot of Mount Carmel, at the Brook Kishon.
See 1 Kings 18:40

Elijah prayed on the top of Mount Carmel and announced that the three-and-one-half-year drought would end. He then outran Ahab's chariot from Mount Carmel to Jezreel, ten miles away.
See 1 Kings 18:42–46

The prophets used Mount Carmel as a symbol of beauty, fruitfulness, majesty, and prosperity.
See Isaiah 35:2

Divided Kingdom When Carmel is referred to as languishing and withering, it indicates God's judgment is on His land.
See Isaiah 33:9; Amos 1:2; Nahum 1:4

Single Kingdom The prophet Jeremiah compared the grandeur of Nebuchadnezzar to the exalted height of Mount Carmel or Mount Tabor.
See Jeremiah 46:18

Mount Carmel from the Jezreel Valley.

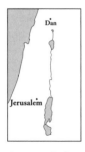

Dan

("judge") The city of Dan was, practically speaking, the northernmost city of Israel in the Old Testament. When the writers of Scripture wanted to speak of all Israel (from north to south), they would say "from Dan to Beersheba" (cf. Judg. 20:1; 1 Sam. 3:20; 2 Sam. 3:10; 17:11; 24:2, 15; 1 Kings 4:25).

Patriarchal Period

Abraham traveled from Hebron to Dan to rescue his nephew Lot from Kedorlaomer.
See Genesis 14:13–16

Period of the Judges

The tribe of Dan was not satisfied with its allotted inheritance near Judah and so settled here, both giving its name to the region and setting up idolatrous worship that plagued Israel throughout its history.
See Judges 18

Divided Kingdom

Jeroboam, the first king of the northern kingdom of Israel, set up golden calves in Dan and Bethel to keep the people from going to Jerusalem to worship.
See 1 Kings 12:26–33

Single Kingdom

The city of Dan symbolized the northern edge of the land, the "gateway" through which Judah's enemies would pass on their way to Jerusalem.
See Jeremiah 4:15; 8:15–16

Platform in the city gate at Dan where the ruler would sit to judge.

Dead Sea

The Dead Sea is approximately 45 miles long, 11 miles wide, and 1,350 feet below sea level, making it the lowest point on the earth's surface. The northern two-thirds of the Dead Sea is extremely deep, reaching a depth of over 1,200 feet, while the southern third is extremely shallow, averaging less than 20 feet. A tongue of land called the Lisan cuts across the Dead Sea from the east, dividing the northern section from the southern third. Were water not being channeled into the salt pans in the south, the entire southern third of the sea would now be dry. In the Bible, the Dead Sea is called the Salt Sea (Num. 34:3, 12), the Sea (Ezek. 47:8), and the eastern sea (Joel 2:20). During the time of Christ, it was also called Lake Asphaltitus. Sodom, Gomorrah, and the "cities of the plain" were located in and around the southern portion of the Dead Sea.

Patriarchal Period	The kings of the east defeated the kings of Sodom and Gomorrah "in the Valley of Siddim (the Salt Sea)." *See Genesis 14:3*
	God "rained down burning sulfur on Sodom and Gomorrah . . . and the entire plain." Abraham's nephew Lot and his daughters escaped, but Lot's wife looked back and became a pillar of salt. *See Genesis 18–19*
Period of the Exodus	God established the Salt Sea as part of Israel's eastern border. *See Numbers 34:3, 12*

United Kingdom	David likely crossed the Dead Sea on the Lisan when he took his family from Judah to Moab to protect them from King Saul. David returned and stayed at "the stronghold" (possibly Masada). *See 1 Samuel 22:3–5*
Divided Kingdom	A combined army from Ammon, Moab, and Edom crossed the Dead Sea at the Lisan to launch a surprise attack against Jerusalem and King Jehoshaphat. God intervened to spare Jerusalem. *See 2 Chronicles 20*
	God promised to remove the locusts (the "northern army") from the land, pushing them into "the eastern sea" (the Dead Sea) and "the western sea" (the Mediterranean Sea). *See Joel 2:20*
Single Kingdom	Jeremiah compared those who trusted in human alliances, rather than God, to a bush dwelling near the Dead Sea in "the parched places of the desert, in a salt land where no one lives." *See Jeremiah 17:6*
	Ezekiel predicted a time when the Dead Sea would become fresh and when fishermen would line its banks. *See Ezekiel 47:8–11*

Ebal (Mount)

(EE bahl) Mount Ebal, rising nearly 3,100 feet above sea level, sits on the northern side of the biblical city of Shechem (modern Nablus). With its twin peak, Mount Gerizim, to the south, these two mountains form a natural valley that leads west from Shechem toward the Mediterranean coast. Mount Ebal is known as the mount of cursing because the curses of God's Law were recited from its slopes. For more information, see Gerizim (Mount) and Shechem.

Period of the Exodus
God commanded Israel to travel to Mount Ebal and Mount Gerizim to recite the blessings and cursings of the covenant once they entered the Promised Land. The cursings were to be recited from Mount Ebal.
See Deuteronomy 11:29

God commanded Israel to build an altar and set up pillars inscribed with the words of His Law on Mount Ebal. He also identified the tribes who were to stand on Mount Ebal and those who were to stand on Mount Gerizim.
See Deuteronomy 27:1–8, 12–13

Period of Conquest
Joshua led the Israelites to Mount Ebal and Mount Gerizim to recite the blessings and cursings of the Law as God had commanded. Joshua also built the altar and set up the pillars inscribed with the words of the Law on Mount Ebal.
See Joshua 8:30–35

Life of Christ
The "woman at the well" whom Jesus met in Samaria was from the village of Sychar located on the slopes of Mount Ebal.
See John 4:4–6

Elath/Ezion Geber

(ee LAHT, ee zih ahn GHEE buhr) Elath was a coastal city at the northern end of the eastern finger of the Red Sea that jutted up from the Sinai peninsula. Elath and the adjacent city of Ezion Geber served as port cities for trade with the Arabian peninsula and Africa.

Period of the Exodus

Israel traveled by Elath and Ezion Geber as they circled around the land of Edom on their way to the east of the Jordan River.
See Numbers 33:35–36; Deuteronomy 2:8

United Kingdom

King Solomon built a fleet of ships at Ezion Geber to sail to Ophir.
See 1 Kings 9:26–28; 2 Chronicles 8:17–18

Divided Kingdom

King Jehoshaphat built a fleet of ships at Ezion Geber to sail to Ophir, but they were destroyed.
See 1 Kings 22:48; 2 Chronicles 20:35–37

King Azariah (Uzziah) recaptured Elath and restored it to Judah's control.
See 2 Kings 14:22; 2 Chronicles 26:1–2

King Rezin of Aram conquered Elath and drove Judah out.
See 2 Kings 16:6

En Gedi

(en GED ee, "spring of the goat")En Gedi is an oasis in the Judean wilderness on the western shore of the Dead Sea. Because of its warm climate and abundant supply of water, the site developed a reputation for its fragrant plants and date palm groves.

Period of Conquest

God allotted En Gedi to the tribe of Judah.
See Joshua 15:62

United Kingdom

David hid in a cave at En Gedi when running from Saul.
See 1 Samuel 23:29

Saul entered the cave where David and his men were hiding, and David cut off part of Saul's robe while Saul "relieved himself."
See 1 Samuel 24

Certain psalms may have been composed at En Gedi by David.
See Psalms 57; 142

Solomon's beloved compared him to "a cluster of henna blossoms" growing in the vineyards of En Gedi.
See Song of Songs 1:14

Divided Kingdom

The Moabites, Ammonites, and Edomites united together at En Gedi to launch a surprise attack against Jerusalem. (En Gedi is the "back door" to Jerusalem from the Dead Sea.) God miraculously intervened to have these nations attack each other instead of Jerusalem.
See 2 Chronicles 20:1–30

Divided Kingdom

Someday in the future, fishermen will line the shores of the Dead Sea "from En Gedi to En Eglaim" to fish.
See Ezekiel 47:10

The refreshing waterfall at En Gedi.

Galilee (Sea of)

The Sea of Galilee is 13 miles long, 7 1/2 miles wide at its northern end, 130–157 feet deep, 32 miles in circumference, and 650 feet below sea level. In the Bible, it is called the Sea of Kinnereth (Num. 34:11; Deut. 3:17; Josh. 13:27; 19:35), the Lake of Gennesaret (Luke 5:1), the Sea of Tiberias (John 21:1), and the Sea of Galilee (Matt. 4:18; 15:29; Mark 1:16; 7:31; John 6:1). Technically, this body of water should be more properly described as a lake than a sea.

Period of Conquest	The mountain range on the eastern shore of the Sea of Kinnereth (Sea of Galilee) was to be the eastern boundary of the Promised Land. *See Numbers 34:11*
Life of Christ	The Sea of Galilee yielded two large catches of fish in response to the command of Christ. *See Luke 5:4–11; John 21:6–8*
	Jesus healed a leper near the Sea of Galilee as He came down from a mountain on His way to Capernaum. *See Matthew 8:1–4*
	Jesus stilled the storm on the Sea of Galilee. *See Matthew 8:23–27; Mark 4:35–41; Luke 8:22–25*
	Demons, cast out of the demoniac by Christ, entered two thousand swine, which plunged into the Sea of Galilee from a steep bank on the eastern shore. *See Matthew 8:28–34; Mark 5:1–21; Luke 8:26–39*

Life of Christ

Jesus walked on the water to the disciples who were struggling in their boat.
See Matthew 14:22–33; Mark 6:45–52; John 6:16–21

Jesus said it would be better to have a millstone tied around one's neck and be drowned in the sea than to cause one who believes in Him to sin. Since Jesus spoke these words in Capernaum (Matt. 17:24), the "sea" He spoke of was likely the Sea of Galilee.
See Matthew 18:1–6

Jesus met the disciples on the shore of the Sea of Galilee after His resurrection.
See John 21

A calm Sea of Galilee at dusk with snow-capped Mount Hermon in the distance.

Gerizim (Mount)

(GEHR uh zeem) Mount Gerizim, at 2,900 feet above sea level, stands slightly lower than its counterpart to the north, Mount Ebal. Both tower over the biblical city of Shechem (modern Nablus). These two mountains form a natural valley that leads west from Shechem to the Mediterranean coast. Mount Gerizim is known as the mount of blessing because the blessings of God's Law were recited from its slopes. During the intertestamental period, the Samaritans erected a temple on Mount Gerizim to rival the Jewish temple in Jerusalem. This temple was destroyed by John Hyrcanus in 129 B.C. This fueled the continuing animosity between the Jews and the Samaritans. For more information, see Ebal (Mount) and Shechem.

Period of the Exodus	God commanded Israel to travel to Mount Ebal and Mount Gerizim to recite the blessings and cursings of the covenant once they entered the Promised Land. The blessings were to be recited from Mount Gerizim. *See Deuteronomy 11:29*
	God identified the tribes who were to stand on Mount Ebal and those who were to stand on Mount Gerizim to recite the blessings and cursings. *See Deuteronomy 27:12–13*
Period of Conquest	Joshua led the Israelites to Mount Ebal and Mount Gerizim to recite the blessings and cursings of the Law as God had commanded. *See Joshua 8:30–35*

Period of the Judges   Gideon's youngest son, Jotham, stood on Mount Gerizim and delivered a message condemning the city of Shechem for making his one brother king and condoning the killing of his other brothers.
See Judges 9:1–21

Life of Christ   The "woman at the well" whom Jesus met in Samaria pointed to Mount Gerizim when she declared, "Our fathers worshiped on this mountain."
See John 4:19–24

Looking up at Mount Gerizim from Jacob's well.

Gibeah

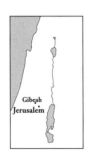

(GIB ee uh) Gibeah, today a hill called Tell el-Ful, was located just three miles north of ancient Jerusalem. The city received its dubious reputation because of its immorality (which started the Benjamite war in the Book of Judges) and because it was the hometown of King Saul, Israel's first king who was rejected by God.

Period of Conquest   Gibeah was assigned to the tribe of Benjamin.
See Joshua 18:28

Period of the Judges   The men of Gibeah raped and killed a Levite's concubine, bringing shame on the nation.
See Judges 19:10–26

The tribe of Benjamin was nearly wiped out from the civil war that resulted when the Benjamites refused to turn over the men of Gibeah who had sinned.
See Judges 20:1–48

United Kingdom   Saul, Israel's first king, came from Gibeah. After his anointing as king, the city was known as "Gibeah of Saul."
See 1 Samuel 10:26; 11:4

During his early conflicts with the Philistines, Saul frequently positioned his forces in or near Gibeah.
See 1 Samuel 13:2, 15; 14:2, 16

United Kingdom	David allowed the Gibeonites to kill seven sons of Saul in Gibeah because of Saul's treachery against them. *See 2 Samuel 21:4–9*
Single Kingdom	The inhabitants of Gibeah fled their village when the Assyrian army marched on Jerusalem in 701 B.C. Gibeah fell to the Assyrians. *See Isaiah 10:31; Hosea 5:8*

Watchtower in field.

Gibeon

(GIB ee uhn) Ancient Gibeon watched over the upper end of the main road from the coastal plain into the hill country. The city, while under Israelite control, was inhabited by the Hivites, who had tricked Joshua into making a peace treaty with them. The modern Arab village of el-Jib preserves the name of ancient Gibeon.

Period of Conquest

The Gibeonites tricked Joshua into making a peace treaty with them, thus allowing them to live in the land as Israel's servants. Five kings of southern Canaan attacked Gibeon when they heard of the Gibeonite treaty with Israel. Joshua marched his army from Gilgal, attacked the armies that had surrounded Gibeon, and defeated them. *See Joshua 9–10*

Gibeon and the surrounding land was allotted to the Levites as one of their forty-eight cities in the land of Israel. *See Joshua 21:17*

United Kingdom

Joab and David's forces met Abner and Ishbosheth's forces at the pool of Gibeon, and David's men won. *See 2 Samuel 2:12–17*

David allowed the Gibeonites to kill seven sons of Saul in Gibeah because of Saul's treachery against them. *See 2 Samuel 21:4–9*

United Kingdom	After becoming king, Solomon offered sacrifices to the Lord at Gibeon and asked for wisdom. God promised him wisdom as well as riches and honor. *See 1 Kings 3:4; 2 Chronicles 1:3–13*
	The tabernacle of the Lord was at Gibeon before Solomon constructed the temple in Jerusalem. (This explains why Solomon went to Gibeon to worship in 1 Kings 3:4.) *See 1 Chronicles 16:37–43; 21:28–30*
Single Kingdom	Hananiah, the false prophet who opposed Jeremiah, was from Gibeon. *See Jeremiah 28:1*
Babylonian Captivity	Jeremiah and the other captives from Mizpah were rescued by the pool of Gibeon. *See Jeremiah 41:11–12*
Restoration	Ninety-five men returned from the Babylonian captivity to their ancestral home in Gibeon. They also helped rebuild the walls of Jerusalem. *See Nehemiah 3:7; 7:25*

The pool at ancient Gibeon with a spiral staircase leading down to the water level.

Gilboa (Mount)

(gil BOH uh) Mount Gilboa is an extended ridge that rises on the southeastern side of the Jezreel Valley. The mountain marked the northernmost edge of the territory assigned to the tribe of Manasseh. Mount Gilboa offered strategic high ground to the Israelite army when facing foreign invaders in the Valley of Jezreel.

Period of the Judges

Gideon chose his three hundred men at the spring of Harod that flows from the base of Mount Gilboa (also called Mount Gilead in 7:3).
See Judges 7

United Kingdom

King Saul and his army camped on Mount Gilboa when they mobilized to fight the Philistines in the Jezreel Valley. The Philistines defeated Israel and killed Saul and his sons on Mount Gilboa.
See 1 Samuel 28:4–5; 31:1–5

David lamented Saul's death and wished Mount Gilboa would become dry and barren because of the tragedy that had occurred on its slopes.
See 2 Samuel 1:21

Mount Gilboa in the distance.

Hazor

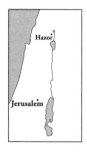

(HOT zor) Hazor was to Israel in the Old Testament what Capernaum was to Israel in the New Testament. It was a strategic city because it was located on a well-defended hill that straddled the International Highway at a spot where it narrowed along the Jordan River. Thus, it served as a first line of defense against armies attacking from the north. It also guarded the trade routes and could thus be used to collect taxes and duties.

Period of Conquest Joshua captured the city from Jabin, king of Hazor, and burned it. At this time, it had a population of approximately forty thousand and was the largest city in the country. *See Joshua 11:1–13*

Period of the Judges Hazor was rebuilt by another ruler named Jabin, who controlled the northern section of Israel for twenty years. This was the judgment of God on Israel for its sins: "The LORD sold them into the hands of Jabin, a king of Canaan, who reigned in Hazor" (Judg. 4:2). Under Deborah and Barak Israel won a great victory over Sisera, Jabin's general, in the Jezreel Valley. (For more information, see Megiddo.) *See Judges 4–5*

United Kingdom Solomon rebuilt Hazor during his reign to guard the northern approach to the land of Israel. *See 1 Kings 9:15*

Divided Kingdom The inhabitants of Hazor were taken into captivity by Tiglath-Pileser, king of Assyria. *See 2 Kings 15:29*

Hebron/Kiriath Arba/Mamre

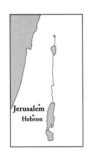

(HEH bruhn, kihr ih at AHR buh, MAM rih)
Ancient Hebron served as the seedbed for the nation
of Israel. Abraham dwelt in Hebron, and the only
land he ever possessed was the burial cave he purchased here. Abraham, Sarah, Isaac, Rebekah, and
Jacob were buried at the cave of Machpelah. Later, David ruled as
king over Judah from Hebron. The remains of the shrine built over
the cave of Machpelah by Herod the Great still stand in Hebron.

Patriarchal Period	Abram settled at "the great trees of Mamre at Hebron." *See Genesis 13:18* Abram marched from Hebron to pursue the army of Kedorlaomer and rescue his nephew Lot. *See Genesis 14:11–16* God's heavenly messengers paid a visit to Abraham at Hebron, and he haggled over the future of Sodom. *See Genesis 18:1–33* Abraham viewed the destruction of Sodom from near Hebron. *See Genesis 19:27–29* Sarah died in "Kiriath Arba (that is, Hebron)," and Abraham purchased the cave of Machpelah as a family burial plot. *See Genesis 23:1–20*

Patriarchal Period

Abraham died and was buried with Sarah in the cave of Machpelah in Hebron.
See Genesis 25:7–10

Isaac died and was buried at the cave of Machpelah in Hebron.
See Genesis 35:27–29

Jacob was buried at the cave of Machpelah in Hebron.
See Genesis 49:29–33; 50:12–14

Period of Conquest

The king of Hebron joined the coalition that opposed Joshua and attacked Gibeon. Joshua attacked Hebron and killed its inhabitants.
See Joshua 10

Caleb personally requested the area surrounding Hebron as his tribal inheritance, driving out the remaining inhabitants.
See Joshua 14:6–15; 15:13–14

Hebron was named as one of the six cities of refuge in the land of Israel.
See Joshua 20:1–9

The Levites were given Hebron as one of their forty-eight cities of inheritance throughout the land of Israel, but the fields and surrounding villages belonged to Caleb and his descendants.
See Joshua 21:11–12

Period of the Judges

Samson carried the city gates of Gaza to Hebron.
See Judges 16:1–3

United Kingdom	David sent some of the spoils of war to Hebron and other cities he had visited as a fugitive from Saul. *See 1 Samuel 30:26–31*
	David was anointed king over Judah at Hebron. *See 2 Samuel 2:1–4, 11*
	Absalom conspired against his father David to take over the kingdom and was anointed king in Hebron. *See 2 Samuel 15:1–12*
Divided Kingdom	King Rehoboam of Judah fortified Hebron for the defense of his kingdom. *See 2 Chronicles 11:10*

The tomb of the patriarchs at Hebron built over the traditional site of the Cave of Machpelah.

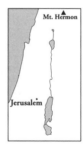

Hermon (Mount)

(HUHR muhn, "sacred mountain") Mount Hermon, on the northeastern fringe of ancient Israel, rises majestically to a height of over nine thousand feet. The mountain stood as a symbol of beauty, fertility, and abundance. Some believe this is the Mount of Transfiguration.

Period of the Exodus
Israel defeated Og, king of Bashan, whose kingdom stretched "as far as Mount Hermon."
See Deuteronomy 3:8–11

Period of Conquest
Mount Hermon marked the northern limits of Joshua's conquests.
See Joshua 11:3, 17; 12:1, 5; 13:5, 11

United Kingdom
Mount Hermon was used in poetry by David and Solomon. Its height and beauty symbolized a place of joy and fruitfulness.
See Psalm 133:3; Song of Songs 4:8

Divided Kingdom
Psalmists saw Mount Hermon picturing God's majesty or standing as the silent sentinel on the edge of God's Promised Land.
See Psalms 42:6; 89:12

Life of Christ
Mount Hermon is considered by many to be the "Mount of Transfiguration" because of its height. (Matthew 17:1 and Mark 9:2 speak of a "high mountain," and Mount Hermon rises over 9,000 feet as compared with Mount Tabor, which is only 1,843 feet.)
See Matthew 17:1–9; Mark 9:2–9;
Luke 9:28–37

Herodium

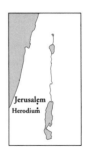

(heh ROH dih uhm) Within viewing distance of Bethlehem stands the Herodium, one of Herod the Great's palace/fortresses that became his place of burial. It is ironic that the "king by might" was buried just a short distance from the birthplace of the "King by Right," whom Herod had tried so hard to destroy. From the Herodium, one can see the towers on the Mount of Olives to the northwest, the village of Bethlehem to the west, and the Judean wilderness and Dead Sea to the east. This is the wilderness in which David shepherded his flocks as a boy (cf. Ps. 23).

A view inside the Heroduim.

The famous sillouette of the Herodium against the Israeli sky.

Jericho

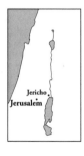

("place of fragrance," "moon-city") Archaeological excavations have shown that civilization existed in Jericho from very ancient times. It is one of the world's oldest cities. The site became so important because of its warm climate, abundant springs of water, and strategic location astride a point where caravans could travel east to west along the Jordan Valley.

Period of Conquest	The spies were received and hidden in Jericho by Rahab. *See Joshua 2*
	Joshua captured Jericho by marching around it seven days. Rahab and her family were spared. *See Joshua 6*
Period of the Judges	Eglon, king of Moab, oppressed Israel and ruled from Jericho, which was called "the City of Palms" (Judg. 3:13). He was defeated by Ehud. *See Judges 3:12–30*
United Kingdom	After David's envoy to the Ammonites had been publicly humiliated, they waited at Jericho until their beards had grown back. *See 2 Samuel 10:4–5*
Divided Kingdom	Jericho was rebuilt as a city in the time of Ahab, king of Israel. The builder sacrificed two of his sons to the false gods in an attempt to guarantee their favor in his task, thus fulfilling Joshua's prediction (Josh. 6:26). *See 1 Kings 16:34*
Divided Kingdom	Elijah and Elisha ministered in Jericho, and both crossed the Jordan River on dry ground

nearby. The bitter water was made pure by Elisha at Jericho.
See 2 Kings 2:4–22

Round Neolithic (New Stone Age) defense (or gate) tower at Old Testament Jericho, from ca. 7000 B.C.

Babylonian Captivity	After Jerusalem's fall to the Babylonians in 586 B.C., King Zedekiah fled from Jerusalem through the Judean wilderness toward the Jordan Valley. He was captured by the Babylonians on the "plains of Jericho."

See 2 Kings 25:4–6; Jeremiah 39:4–6

Restoration During the return from Babylon, 345 men from Jericho made the journey back to their hometown. They also helped rebuild the walls of Jerusalem.
See Ezra 2:34; Nehemiah 3:2; 7:36

Life of Christ Herod the Great built his palace and administrative buildings approximately one mile south of the mound on which Old Testament Jericho had been built. The "new" city of Jericho served as one of Herod the Great's winter palaces.

Jesus was tempted by Satan in the Judean wilderness. The traditional site of this temptation is the nearby Mount of Temptation.
See Matthew 4:1–11; Mark 1:12–13; Luke 4:1–13

Zacchaeus was converted in Jericho after Jesus spotted him in a sycamore-fig tree.
See Luke 19:1–10

Life of Christ Christ healed blind Bartimaeus and his companion in Jericho during His final trip to Jerusalem.
See Matthew 20:29–34; Mark 10:46–52; Luke 18:35–43

Jerusalem

(jih ROO suh lem) Jerusalem, the capital of ancient Israel, stands as one of the most important cities in all the world. But its importance comes ultimately from God. It is "the city the LORD had chosen . . . in which to put His Name" (1 Kings 14:21; see also 2 Chron. 6:6). From its selection as "the City of David" to the eternal glory of the "new Jerusalem," this city occupies a primary place in God's work on earth.

Patriarchal Period	Abram paid tithes to Melchizedek (whose name means "my king is righteousness") in the city of Salem. *See Genesis 14:17–24*
	Abraham prepared to offer Isaac on Mount Moriah, the mountain on the northern edge of ancient Jerusalem, which is now covered by the Dome of the Rock. *See Genesis 22*
Period of Conquest	Joshua defeated Adoni-Zedek, king of Jerusalem. *See Joshua 10:1–11*

The tribe of Judah captured Jerusalem and killed its inhabitants, but apparently they did not occupy the city that was soon reoccupied by the Jebusites (Judg. 1:21). *See Judges 1:1, 8*

A tomb, possibly dating from as early as the first century A.D., in the city of Jerusalem.

Period of the Judges

Jerusalem was known as "Jebus" and the "city of the Jebusites."
See Judges 19:10–11

United Kingdom

David captured, strengthened, and beautified the city, making it his capital. (David reigned seven and one-half years in Hebron and thirty-three years in Jerusalem, 1010–970 B.C.) David called Jerusalem "the City of David" (2 Sam. 5:9). The city at that time occupied only the cone-shaped spur of land south of the temple mount that is outside the present-day city walls.
See 2 Samuel 5:5–16

David brought the ark of the covenant to Jerusalem.
See 2 Samuel 6:1–12

David purchased the threshing floor of Araunah the Jebusite, which later became the site of Solomon's temple.
See 2 Samuel 24:18–25; 2 Chronicles 3:1

David was buried in Jerusalem.
See 1 Kings 2:10

Solomon, who reigned 970–931 B.C., built the temple and other magnificent buildings. He expanded the city of Jerusalem north so that it included the original city of David and Mount Moriah.
See 1 Kings 6–9

Divided Kingdom

Shishak, king of Egypt, attacked and plundered Jerusalem in 926 B.C. during the reign of Rehoboam, son of Solomon.
See 1 Kings 14:25–28

The Philistines and Arabs attacked and plundered Jerusalem about 845 B.C. during the reign of Jehoram. This attack could be the basis for Obadiah's prophecy.
See 2 Chronicles 21:16–17

The northern kingdom of Israel attacked and plundered Jerusalem (and tore down a section of its walls) about 785 B.C. during the reign of Amaziah.
See 2 Chronicles 25:17–24

Single Kingdom

Sennacherib, king of Assyria, surrounded Jerusalem in 701 B.C. King Hezekiah went to Isaiah to ask for the Lord's deliverance, and God killed 185,000 Assyrian troops, sparing Jerusalem from attack. Sometime just prior to this invasion, Hezekiah had expanded the city of Jerusalem to include the Western Hill (today mistakenly called "Mount Zion"). The city had greatly expanded in size because of the influx of refugees following the fall of the northern kingdom of Israel to Assyria in 722 B.C. Hezekiah also constructed the Pool of Siloam and dug a water tunnel ("Hezekiah's tunnel") to channel the water of the Gihon Spring into the Pool of Siloam.
See 2 Kings 18; 2 Chronicles 32:30; Isaiah 36–37

Babylonian Captivity   After a thirty-month siege, Nebuchadnezzar of Babylon captured, sacked, and burned Jerusalem in 586 B.C.
See 2 Kings 25:1–3; Jeremiah 39:1–3

After Jerusalem's fall to the Babylonians in 586 B.C., King Zedekiah fled from Jerusalem through the Judean wilderness toward the Jordan Valley. He was captured by the Babylonians on the plains of Jericho.
See 2 Kings 25:4–6; Jeremiah 39:4–6

Restoration   Under Zerubbabel, almost fifty thousand Jews returned from Babylon in 537 B.C. and laid the foundation of the temple in 536. After a sixteen-year delay, they resumed work on the temple in 520 B.C. and completed it in 516. Ezra journeyed to Jerusalem in 457 B.C.
See Ezra 1–6

Nehemiah rebuilt the walls of Jerusalem about 444 B.C. Some parts of his walls can still be seen along the eastern ridge of the original city of David.
See Nehemiah 1–6

Intertestamental Era   Alexander the Great captured Jerusalem in 332 B.C. Tradition says the city was spared when the high priest showed Alexander the prophecies of Daniel that predicted Alexander's rise to power. In 167 B.C., Antiochus Epiphanes defiled the temple and dedicated it to the worship of Zeus. The Jews rebelled under the leadership of an aged priest named Mattathias and his sons. One son, Judas Maccabeus, recaptured Jerusalem and purified the temple in 164 B.C. The Jewish feast of Hanukkah commemorates this event.

Intertestament Era

The Roman general Pompey captured Jerusalem and established Roman control of Judea in 63 B.C. Herod the Great built his temple in Jerusalem, starting in 20 B.C.

Life of Christ

Jesus was presented at the temple as an infant and visited the temple at age twelve.
See Luke 2:22, 27, 41–52

Twice, at the opening and the closing of His ministry, Jesus cleansed the temple.
See John 2:12–25; Luke 19:45–48

Jesus healed a man at the pool of Bethesda in Jerusalem.
See John 5:7–10

Jesus rode down the Mount of Olives to Jerusalem and made His formal presentation to Israel as the Messiah.
See Matthew 21:1–11; Mark 11:1–11; Luke 19:28–44; John 12:12–19

On the Mount of Olives, Jesus delivered the Olivet Discourse and foretold the destruction of the temple.
See Matthew 24–25

In an upper room Jesus washed the disciples' feet, instituted the Lord's Supper, and delivered the Upper Room Discourse.
See John 13–16

Life of Christ	Jesus was tried, crucified, buried, and resurrected in Jerusalem. His final ascension to heaven took place just east of Jerusalem on the Mount of Olives. *See Matthew 27–28; Mark 15–16;* *Luke 23–24; John 19–20*
Apostolic Age	The Holy Spirit descended on the disciples who were gathered in Jerusalem on the day of Pentecost, and the church was born. *See Acts 2* Peter and the other apostles preached at the temple. *See Acts 3:2, 11; 5:21* Stephen was martyred in Jerusalem. *See Acts 7* Saul left Jerusalem for Damascus and was converted. *See Acts 9* The first church council convened in Jerusalem. *See Acts 15* Paul, after his third missionary journey, visited Jerusalem, where he was seized by the Jews during a visit to the temple. *See Acts 21:17–23; 23*

POST-APOSTOLIC HISTORY OF JERUSALEM:

Roman Era
(63 B.C.–A.D. 330) The Roman general Titus destroyed Jerusalem in A.D. 70. It was destroyed again by Emperor Hadrian in A.D. 135 following the Bar Kochba revolt. Hadrian rebuilt the city and renamed it Aelia Capitolina. The street called the Cardo (and the overall layout of Jerusalem today) dates to this period.

Byzantine Era
(A.D. 330–634)

Arab Era
(634–1099)

Crusader Period
(1099–1187; 1229–1244)

Arab Era
(1187–1517 except 1229–1244)

Turkish Era
(1517–1917). The present city walls were built by Suleiman I [the Magnificent] who reigned from 1520 to 1566.

British Era
(1917–1948)

Jordanian Era
(1948–1967)

Israeli Independence
(1967–)

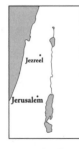

Jezreel

(JEZ reel, "God sows") The city of Jezreel sits on the northwestern edge of Mount Gilboa overlooking the Jezreel Valley. The valley likely took its name from the city.

Period of Conquest

God allotted the city of Jezreel to the tribe of Issachar.
See Joshua 19:18

Divided Kingdom

Elijah outran Ahab's chariot from Mount Carmel to Jezreel.
See 1 Kings 18:45–46

Ahab and Jezebel coveted and seized the vineyard of Naboth in Jezreel. Elijah condemned their murder of Naboth and predicted God's destruction of their royal line.
See 1 Kings 21:1–19

The kings of Israel and Judah returned from battle to rest and recuperate at Jezreel. Jehu rode up the valley from the Jordan River and killed both kings as well as Queen Jezebel.
See 2 Kings 8:28–29; 9:14–37

Jehu massacred all Ahab's descendants at Jezreel. The prophet Hosea condemned this bloodshed.
See 2 Kings 10:1–11; Hosea 1:4

Jezreel (Valley of)

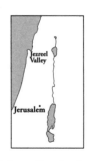

(JEZ reel, "God sows") The arrowhead-shaped Valley of Jezreel is an apt stage for the historical dramas played out on its floor. The valley served as a crossroads, with the International Highway from Egypt to Mesopotamia intersecting a major east-west road from the Mediterranean Sea to the Jordan Valley and beyond. To understand the importance of the valley, look up the cities and mountains that ring this stage. Those included in this book are Beth Shan, Mount Carmel, Mount Gilboa, the city of Jezreel, Megiddo, the hill of Moreh, Nazareth, and Mount Tabor.

Period of Conquest	God allotted the Valley of Jezreel to the tribe of Manasseh, but they could not take it because the inhabitants of the valley used "chariots of iron." *See Joshua 17:16*
Period of the Judges	Gideon defeated the Midianites in the Valley of Jezreel. Gideon and his men camped on Mount Gilboa while the Philistines camped on the hill of Moreh. *See Judges 6:33–37; 7:1–25*
United Kingdom	Saul was killed by the Philistines on Mount Gilboa at the southeastern end of the Valley of Jezreel. *See 1 Samuel 29:1; 31:1–8*
	Solomon placed Beth Shan, Megiddo, and Jezreel under the governorship of Baana, son of Ahilud. *See 1 Kings 4:12*

Divided Kingdom

Ahab and Jezebel had a residence in the city of Jezreel that is in the Valley of Jezreel. After the contest with the prophets of Baal on Mount Carmel, Elijah outran Ahab's chariot to Jezreel, where Jezebel threatened to have him killed.
See 1 Kings 18:45–19:2

Ahab and Jezebel had Naboth killed so they could "appropriate" his land and vineyard in Jezreel for themselves.
See 1 Kings 21:1–24

The prophet Elisha raised the Shunammite woman's son back to life. (Shunem is located in the Jezreel Valley on the southern slope of the hill of Moreh.)
See 2 Kings 4:8–37

Jehu killed Joram, king of Israel (Ahab's son); Ahaziah, king of Judah; and Jezebel in Jezreel.
See 2 Kings 9:14–37

The prophet Hosea named his first child "Jezreel" as a sign to show Israel that God would allow them to be defeated in the Jezreel Valley for the bloodshed of Jehu and his successors at the city of Jezreel.
See Hosea 1:4–5

Joppa/Jaffa/Tel Aviv

(JAH puh, JAF fuh, tel uh VEEV) The port city of
Joppa (modern Jaffa) served as Israel's link to the sea
throughout the Old Testament. Today, the city of Tel
Aviv sits on the north side of Jaffa and dwarfs Israel's
ancient seaport.

Period of Conquest	God allotted the city of Joppa to the tribe of Dan, but they failed to capture it. *See Joshua 19:46–47*
United Kingdom	During Solomon's reign, Joppa served as the chief seaport of Jerusalem. Cedars from Lebanon were floated down to Joppa and then transported to Jerusalem for the building of the temple. *See 2 Chronicles 2:16*
Divided Kingdom	Jonah sailed from Joppa when he tried to flee to Tarshish rather than obey God's command to go to Nineveh. *See Jonah 1:3*
Restoration	Cedars from Lebanon were again floated down to Joppa for the rebuilding of the temple. *See Ezra 3:7*
Apostolic Age	Peter raised Dorcas to life at Joppa. *See Acts 9:36–43*
	Peter had a vision on the housetop of Simon the tanner in Joppa showing him God wanted him to share His "good news" with the Gentiles. This led to Peter's ministry in the house of Cornelius at Caesarea. *See Acts 10*

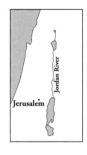

Jordan River

The Jordan River (meaning "go down") flows from the Sea of Galilee to the Dead Sea. Although the actual distance between these two bodies of water is less than 70 miles, the Jordan River snakes along in a winding path that gives the river a final length of almost 110 miles. There were some settlements along the river (notably Beth Shan in the north and Jericho in the south), but the area was not generally favorable for settlement. Instead, much of the area along the Jordan River was covered with dense vegetation that hid wild animals (see Jer. 12:5; 49:19; 50:44). Today the Jordan River is not impressive. It is actually a small stream less than fifty feet wide most of the year. Much of the water that once fed the Jordan River is now used for irrigation.

Patriarchal Period Lot chose the "plain of the Jordan" near Jericho when he and his family separated from Abram. Lot selected the area because it was "well watered . . . like the land of Egypt." Lot later moved to Sodom and Gomorrah.
See Genesis 13:10–11

Period of the Exodus God identified the Jordan River as the eastern border of Israel.
See Numbers 34:10–12

Period of Conquest Just before entering the Promised Land, the Israelites camped on the plains of Moab by the Jordan River.
See Numbers 22:1

Period of Conquest

Joshua led Israel across the Jordan River while God stopped the waters upstream at the town of Adam.
See Joshua 3:1–4:18

Period of the Judges

Ehud and the Israelites seized control of the "fords of the Jordan" to cut off Moab's escape. Controlling this strategic crossing point allowed them to destroy Moab's occupying army.
See Judges 3:28–30

Gideon and the Israelites seized control of the "waters of the Jordan" to prohibit the Midianites from escaping across the river.
See Judges 7:24–25

Jephthah and the Israelites of Gilead fought against the tribe of Ephraim. In the battle, Jephthah's men seized the "fords of the Jordan" and killed the soldiers of Ephraim who tried to escape.
See Judges 12:1–7

United Kingdom

Following the Philistines' defeat of Saul, the Israelites along the northern Jordan valley fled. The Philistines occupied the land, including the city of Beth Shan.
See 1 Samuel 31:7–10

When Absalom rebelled against his father, David, King David fled across the Jordan River to escape his son's army.
See 2 Samuel 17:15–22

United Kingdom	The large bronze objects for Solomon's temple were cast in clay molds "in the plain of the Jordan." *See 2 Chronicles 4:16–17*
Divided Kingdom	Elijah and Elisha crossed the Jordan on dry ground. After Elijah's translation into heaven, Elisha repeated the miracle on his return into the land of Israel. *See 2 Kings 2:7–14*

Divided Kingdom

Elijah and Elisha crossed the Jordan on dry ground. After Elijah's translation into heaven, Elisha repeated the miracle on his return into the land of Israel.
See 2 Kings 2:7–14

The Syrian general, Naaman, was healed of leprosy after obeying Elisha's orders and dipping himself seven times in the Jordan River.
See 2 Kings 5:9–15

Elisha caused an axhead to float after it had fallen into the Jordan River.
See 2 Kings 6:3–7

The psalmist remembered God's great miracle in turning back the waters of the Jordan River.
See Psalm 114:3–5

Micah reminded the Israelites of their journey "from Shittim to Gilgal," a reference to their journey through the Jordan River on dry ground.
See Micah 6:5

Single Kingdom

God rebuked Jeremiah by warning him that if he was having trouble now (in the "safe country"), the going would become more difficult (in the "thickets by the Jordan").
See Jeremiah 12:5

Single Kingdom

Lions lived among the thick vegetation along the Jordan River.
See Jeremiah 49:19; 50:44

Babylonian Captivity

God again identified the Jordan River as the eastern border of Israel.
See Ezekiel 47:18

Restoration

Lions lived among the thick vegetation along the Jordan River.
See Zechariah 11:3

Life of Christ

John the Baptist baptized in the Jordan River.
See Matthew 3:5–6; Mark 1:5; John 1:28

Jesus was baptized in the Jordan River.
See Matthew 3:13–17; Mark 1:9

Jesus "went back across the Jordan" to the location where John the Baptist had first been baptizing.
See John 10:40–42

The waters of the Jordan River as it meanders through Israel.

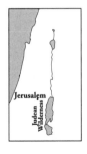

Judean Wilderness

The Judean wilderness extends from just north of Jerusalem to the southern tip of the Dead Sea. The strip of land itself is approximately 10–20 miles wide and lies between the hill country of Judah and the Rift Valley. This land is in the "rain shadow"—that area on the east side of the hill country that receives little rain from the Mediterranean Sea. The area experiences a tremendous drop in elevation. From Jerusalem to Jericho (a distance of approximately 13 miles) the land drops from 2,600 feet above sea level to 1,100 feet below sea level—a drop of 3,700 feet! In the Old Testament, individual portions of the Judean wilderness were often named for nearby towns and villages (such as the Desert of En Gedi, the Desert of Maon, the Desert of Tekoa, and the Desert of Ziph).

Period of Conquest	The Israelites stoned to death Achan and his family in the "Valley of Achor" for his sin at Jericho. *See Joshua 7:24–26*
	Joshua and the Israelites marched through the Judean wilderness at night as they went from Gilgal to Gibeon to rescue the Gibeonites. *See Joshua 10:7–9*
	Part of the tribal allotment for Judah included the land "in the desert"—a reference to the Judean wilderness. *See Joshua 15:61–63*
Period of the Judges	After the intertribal warfare in Israel, only the six hundred Benjamites who fled "into the desert to the rock of Rimmon" remained alive. *See Judges 20:47*

United Kingdom

David hid from Saul in the "Desert of Ziph."
See 1 Samuel 23:15–29

David spared Saul's life in the "Desert of En Gedi."
See 1 Samuel 24:1–22

In the "Desert of Maon," Nabal refused to help David and was struck dead. David took Abigail to be his wife.
See 1 Samuel 25:1–40

In the "Desert of Ziph," David again spared Saul's life.
See 1 Samuel 26:1–25

Shimei cursed David as he traveled east from Jerusalem through the Judean wilderness to flee Absalom.
See 2 Samuel 16:5–14

The daughters of Jerusalem were summoned to watch Solomon "coming up from the desert" to Jerusalem for his wedding.
See Song of Songs 3:6–11

The Wilderness of Judea.

Divided Kingdom	King Jehoshaphat led his people into the "Desert of Tekoa" to repel a threatened attack against Jerusalem. The invaders were coming from En Gedi. *See 2 Chronicles 20:1–24*
	The prophet Isaiah looked forward to a time when "a voice crying in the wilderness" would announce a message of comfort to Jerusalem. *See Isaiah 40:1–11*
Divided Kingdom	Hosea predicted a time when God would bring the nation of Israel "into the desert" in a second exodus. This time God would make "the Valley of Achor a door of hope" *See Hosea 2:14–15*
Single Kingdom	Jeremiah announced that those who put their trust in people rather than God would be like "a bush in the wastelands" that would dwell in the "parched places of the desert." *See Jeremiah 17:5–8*
	Ezekiel described a time when a permanent stream of living water would flow from Jerusalem toward "the eastern region" to bring life to a barren land. *See Ezekiel 47:8–12*
Babylonian Captivity	After Jerusalem's fall to the Babylonians in 586 B.C., King Zedekiah fled from Jerusalem through the Judean wilderness toward the Jordan Valley. He was captured by the Babylonians on the plains of Jericho. *See 2 Kings 25:4–6; Jeremiah 39:4–6*

Life of Christ

John the Baptist began his ministry in the "Desert of Judea."
See Matthew 3:1–3; Mark 1:4–5; Luke 3:2

After His baptism in the Jordan, Jesus was led into the desert to be tempted for forty days.
See Matthew 4:1–11; Mark 1:12–13; Luke 4:1–13

Jesus' parable of the good Samaritan was set in the Judean wilderness between Jerusalem and Jericho.
See Luke 10:25–37

After raising Lazarus from the dead, Jesus withdrew with His disciples "to a region near the desert, to a village called Ephraim."
See John 11:54

The Wilderness of Judea as viewed toward the Dead Sea (left center) from atop the Herodium.

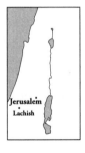

Jerusalem
Lachish

Lachish

(LAY kish) The city of Lachish guarded a major road through Judah's foothills from the coast to the city of Hebron. The city's location and strong natural defenses gave it strategic importance. Ultimately, the city of Lachish became second in importance only to Jerusalem during the latter part of the kingdom of Judah.

Period of Conquest

The king of Lachish joined the coalition that opposed Joshua and attacked Gibeon. Joshua attacked Lachish and killed its inhabitants.
See Joshua 10

God allotted Lachish to the tribe of Judah.
See Joshua 15:39

Divided Kingdom

King Rehoboam of Judah fortified Lachish for the defense of his kingdom.
See 2 Chronicles 11:9

King Amaziah fled from Jerusalem to Lachish to avoid an assassination attempt, but the conspirators went to Lachish and killed him there.
See 2 Kings 14:17–20;
2 Chronicles 25:27–28

Single Kingdom

Sennacherib, king of Assyria, invaded Judah and sent his army against Lachish. The city fell to Sennacherib in 701 B.C. He commemorated the victory with a series of reliefs carved on his palace walls in Nineveh depicting the siege and capture of Lachish.
See 2 Kings 18:14, 17; 19:8;
2 Chronicles 32:9; Isaiah 36:2; 37:8;
Micah 1:13

Single Kingdom

Nebuchadnezzar, king of Babylon, invaded Judah and sent his army against Judah's cities. Near the end of his invasion, only Lachish, Azekah, and Jerusalem remained unconquered. Eventually, all three cities fell. *See Jeremiah 34:7*

Restoration

Some of the remnant who returned from Babylonian captivity reinhabited Lachish. *See Nehemiah 11:30*

Tel Lachish, Judah's dominant city in the low hills of the Shephelah.

Masada

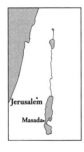

(muh SAH duh) Masada, a natural mesa near the western shore of the Dead Sea, matches well its Hebrew name, "the stronghold" (Hebrew, *metsuda*). Masada is a shrine and symbol of modern Israel. When cadets graduate from Israel's military academy, they swear a proud oath, "Masada shall not fall again!"

United Kingdom

After taking his parents to Moab for safety, David and his four hundred men returned to Judah and temporarily camped "in the stronghold." Some Old Testament scholars identify this location with Masada.
See 1 Samuel 22:3–5; 1 Chronicles 12:1–16

After confronting Saul at En Gedi, David fled to the "stronghold."
See 1 Samuel 24:22

Intertestamental Era

Herod the Great (37–4 B.C.) fortified Masada ("stronghold" or "fortress"), surrounding the top with a wall eighteen feet high. He also built a winter palace here, and the site was considered impregnable.

Apostolic Age

When Jerusalem fell to the Romans in A.D. 70, Jewish patriots, under the leadership of Eliezer Ben Yair, fled to Masada, where they took their final stand against Rome. Finally, on April 15, A.D. 73, the Romans broke into the fortress and found that all of the defenders except two women and five children had killed each other. According to the Jewish historian Josephus, 960 people took their own lives at Masada, choosing death over slavery to Rome.

Megiddo

(mih GID oh, "place of troops") Megiddo lies on the southern end of the Plain of Esdraelon (or the Jezreel Valley), a broad arrowhead-shaped valley that is twenty miles long and fourteen miles wide at its broadest point. The city of Megiddo was very large, and the site guarded a strategic pass through Mount Carmel. Twenty separate layers of occupation were found at Megiddo, each one built on top of the ruins of the preceding city.

Period of Conquest
The king of Megiddo was one of thirty-one kings defeated by Joshua during Israel's conquest of Canaan.
See Joshua 12:7, 21

Period of the Judges
God allotted the city of Megiddo to the tribe of Manasseh, but they failed to drive the Canaanites out.
See Judges 1:27

Deborah and Barak defeated Sisera and his armies "by the waters of Megiddo." These waters are the Kishon River which flows through the Jezreel Valley (cp. Judg. 5:21). The "river" is normally a small stream. Evidently, part of God's miracle was a sudden thunderstorm which caused the stream to overflow its banks (cf. 5:4).
See Judges 5:19–20

United Kingdom	Solomon placed Beth Shan, Megiddo, and Jezreel under the governorship of Baana, son of Ahilud. *See 1 Kings 4:12*
	Solomon fortified the city of Megiddo as an important defense post. *See 1 Kings 9:15; 10:26*
Divided Kingdom	Jehu attacked King Ahaziah of Judah near Jezreel. Ahaziah managed to flee to Megiddo before he died. *See 2 Kings 9:27*
Single Kingdom	Josiah, the last good king of Judah, unwisely tried to stop Pharaoh Neco and the Egyptian army from marching through the land. Josiah failed and was killed at Megiddo in 609 B.C. *See 2 Kings 23:29–30; 2 Chronicles 35:20–24*
Apostolic Age	The last great gathering of armies just before Christ's return to earth will take place at Armageddon. In Hebrew, *Har Megiddo*, means the "Hill of Megiddo." *See Revelation 16:13–16*

Manger and "hitching post" stones likely from a ninth century B.C. stable or building at Megiddo.

Mizpah

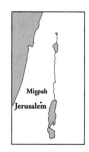

(MITZ pah) At least five different cities or towns in the Bible had the name Mizpah, which means "watchtower." They include (1) Mizpah of Gilead in the Transjordan (present-day northern Jordan) where Jacob and Laban made a covenant (Gen. 31:23–49) and, possibly, where Jephthah the judge later lived (Judg. 11:1, 29, 34); (2) Mizpah in Galilee at the foot of Mount Hermon (Josh. 11:3, 8); (3) Mizpah in Judah in the low foothills near Lachish (Josh. 15:38–39); (4) Mizpah of Moab (present-day central Jordan) where David took his family to protect them from King Saul (1 Sam. 22:3); and (5) Mizpah in Benjamin. This last Mizpah is the one that is most prominent in the Old Testament. The events that occurred there are listed below.

Period of Conquest
God allotted Mizpah to the tribe of Benjamin.
See Joshua 18:26

Period of the Judges
All Israel gathered at Mizpah to judge the sin of the men of Gibeah. This led to the tragic civil war of Judges 20–21.
See Judges 20:1–11

Samuel summoned all Israel to Mizpah for a national convocation to renew their covenant with God. God responded by giving Israel a great victory over the Philistines, who mounted an attack against the Israelites.
See 1 Samuel 7:5–12

United Kingdom   Samuel summoned Israel to Mizpah a second time to witness the selection of Saul as Israel's first king.
See 1 Samuel 10:17–27

Divided Kingdom   King Asa of Judah fortified Mizpah to protect against a threatened attack by King Baasha of Israel.
See 1 Kings 15:16–22; 2 Chronicles 16:1–10

Babylonian Captivity   Mizpah became the seat of government after the destruction of Judah. King Nebuchadnezzar of Babylon appointed Gedaliah governor, and Jeremiah was allowed to live at Mizpah with him. This period ended when Gedaliah was assassinated by a usurper named Ishmael, who took the people of Mizpah captive and forced them to leave.
See Jeremiah 40–41

Aerial view of Nebi Samwil, one possible location of Mizpah.

Moreh (Hill of)

(MOUR ay) The hill of Moreh splits the eastern end of the Jezreel Valley. Though less than 1,700 feet high, the hill's strategic location in the valley near the route of the International Highway gave it some prominence. Four villages situated on or near the hill of Moreh played a significant role in biblical history. These were Ophrah, Shunem, Endor, and Nain.

Period of the Judges

Gideon lived in the town of Ophrah on the southwestern side of the hill of Moreh in the Jezreel Valley. The modern town of Afula preserves the name of Gideon's hometown. *See Judges 6:11, 24*

Gideon fought the Midianites, who camped in the Jezreel Valley near the hill of Moreh. *See Judges 7:1*

United Kingdom

The Philistines camped at the village of Shunem on the southern slope of the hill of Moreh, when they gathered to fight against Saul and the Israelites. Saul secretly visited a medium who lived in Endor, a small village on the northern side of the hill of Moreh. *See 1 Samuel 28:4*

United Kingdom

Abishag the Shunammite (from the village of Shunem on the southern slope of the hill of Moreh) was chosen to take care of King David in his old age. *See 1 Kings 1:3–4*

Divided Kingdom

Elisha often visited the city of Shunem on the hill of Moreh and stayed with a prominent woman and her husband. He promised the woman she would have a son, and he later raised the woman's son to life after the young man had died.

See 2 Kings 4:8–37

Life of Christ

Jesus visited the town of Nain on the northern slope of the hill of Moreh and raised a woman's young son to life. The people responded by shouting, "A great prophet has appeared among us," possibly remembering the miracle of Elisha that occurred almost nine hundred years earlier in the same general area.

See Luke 7:11–17

The hill of Moreh.

Nazareth

(NAZ uh reth) Nazareth, a small village on a ridge overlooking the Jezreel Valley, is never mentioned in the Old Testament. The name comes from the Hebrew word for branch or shoot *(netzer)*. Nazareth became important historically because it was the "hometown" of Jesus.

Life of Christ

The angel Gabriel appeared to Mary in Nazareth and announced that she would be the mother of Jesus.
See Luke 1:26–28

Joseph and Mary left Nazareth and went to Bethlehem, where Jesus was born.
See Luke 2:1–7

After fleeing to Egypt to escape Herod's decree to murder the children of Bethlehem, Joseph, Mary, and Jesus returned to the land and settled in Nazareth.
See Matthew 2:21–23

Jesus' boyhood and young manhood were spent in Nazareth, though every year "his parents went to Jerusalem for the feast of the Passover."
See Luke 2:41–52

After Jesus' baptism in the Jordan River and temptation in the wilderness, He preached His first recorded sermon at Nazareth. The people of Nazareth responded angrily to Jesus' message and tried to kill Him by throwing Him from the "Mount of Precipitation."
See Luke 4:16–30

Life of Christ

On a later visit to Nazareth, Jesus could perform few miracles because of the persistent unbelief of the people.
See Mark 6:1–6

The modern city of Nazareth with the Catholic Church of the Annunciation in the center of photo.

Olives (Mount of)

The Mount of Olives rises to the east of Jerusalem and reaches a height of almost 2,500 feet. Though never part of Jerusalem proper, the Mount of Olives is inseparably linked to Jerusalem geographically and historically. The hill received its name because it was covered with olive groves. Though some olive trees still remain, today the hill is largely covered with Jewish graves and Christian shrines.

United Kingdom	King David walked up the Mount of Olives as he fled Jerusalem to escape from his son Absalom. He ascended the Mount of Olives "weeping as he went; his head was covered and he was barefoot." *See 2 Samuel 15:30–37*
	Solomon built pagan shrines for his many wives on the southern portion of the Mount of Olives. *See 1 Kings 11:7–8*
Single Kingdom	Ezekiel witnessed the glory of the Lord leave Solomon's temple and Jerusalem by way of the Mount of Olives. *See Ezekiel 11:22–23*
Single Kingdom	Ezekiel described the glory of the Lord returning from the east (over the Mount of Olives) to enter a new temple. *See Ezekiel 43:1–5*

Restoration

Zechariah described a day when the Lord's feet would stand on the Mount of Olives and the mountain would be split in two.
See Zechariah 14:3–5

Life of Christ

Jesus rode down the Mount of Olives into Jerusalem on a donkey for His "triumphal entry."
See Matthew 21:1–11; Mark 11:1–10; Luke 19:28–40; John 12:12–16

Jesus wept over Jerusalem from the Mount of Olives.
See Luke 19:41–44

Jesus described the prophetic future of Jerusalem to His disciples while they were seated on the Mount of Olives.
See Matthew 24–25; Mark 13:1–37; Luke 21:5–36

Jesus and His disciples left the Upper Room and went to the Garden of Gethsemane on the Mount of Olives. Here Jesus was arrested.
See Matthew 26:36–56; Mark 14:32–52; Luke 22:39–53; John 18:1–11

Jesus, after His resurrection, ascended to heaven from the Mount of Olives.
See Luke 24:50–53; Acts 1:9–12

The western slope of the Mount of Olives on which Jesus gave His Olivet discourse.

Qumran

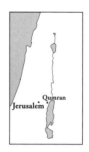

(Koom RAHN) Qumran is located near the northwestern shore of the Dead Sea, and it was the site of a small settlement that existed during the time of Christ. The Dead Sea Scrolls were discovered near Qumran in 1947, and the discovery of these scrolls gave the site its importance. Many (though not all) scholars believe Qumran was inhabited by a Jewish sect called the Essenes. Most likely the Essenes, hearing of the approach of the Roman armies in A.D. 68, placed their scrolls in pottery jars and hid them in the nearby caves, intending to return for them later. The Essenes then joined the rebels who captured Masada. They remained at Masada, where they were killed by the Romans in A.D. 73.

A cave at Qumran where some of the Dead Sea Scrolls were discovered.

Ramah

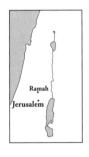

(RAHM ah, "height") Ramah, a strategic village about six miles north of Jerusalem, guarded an important crossroads in the territory of Benjamin. The city sat on the "Way of the Patriarchs," the internal road running through the hill country of Israel, where it intersected the main east-west road that ran from the Mediterranean coast through the hill country to Jericho.

Period of Conquest

God allotted Ramah to the tribe of Benjamin.
See Joshua 18:25

Period of the Judges

The prophetess Deborah sat under a palm tree between Ramah and Bethel to judge Israel.
See Judges 4:5

Elkanah and Hannah resided in Ramah (also called Ramathaim). The prophet Samuel was born in Ramah and lived in Ramah as an adult.
See 1 Samuel 1:1–19; 7:15–17

The people came to Samuel at Ramah to ask for a king. Later, Samuel privately anointed Saul as king in Ramah.
See 1 Samuel 8:4; 9:6, 27; 10:1

United Kingdom

David fled from Saul and visited Samuel at Ramah. Saul pursued David, but God intervened to spare him.
See 1 Samuel 19:18–20:1

United Kingdom   After his death, Samuel was buried at his home in Ramah.
See 1 Samuel 25:1; 28:3

Divided Kingdom   King Baasha of Israel captured and fortified Ramah to block access to Jerusalem. The blockade was lifted and the building materials were removed by King Asa of Judah.
See 1 Kings 15:16–22; 2 Chronicles 16:1–6

Single Kingdom   The inhabitants of Ramah fled in terror when the Assyrian army marched on Jerusalem in 701 B.C. Ramah fell to Sennacherib and the Assyrians.
See Isaiah 10:29; Hosea 5:8

Babylonian Captivity   The Babylonians used Ramah as their "staging area" after the fall of Jerusalem. Captives were taken there for processing before being deported to Babylon. Jeremiah described the women who watched their children being taken into captivity from Ramah as "Rachel weeping for her children."
See Jeremiah 31:15; 40:1

Restoration   Some of the remnant who returned from the Babylonian captivity reinhabited Ramah.
See Ezra 2:26; Nehemiah 7:30

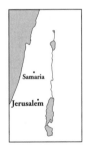

Samaria

(suh MEHR ih uh) The city of Samaria was the final capital of the northern kingdom of Israel. Its strategic location allowed the kings of Israel to exert control out to the Mediterranean coast and the International Highway while protecting key routes into Israel. The city of Samaria was destroyed by the Assyrians in 721 B.C.

Divided Kingdom

King Omri of Israel moved his capital to the city of Samaria.
See 1 Kings 16:23–24

King Ahab built a temple for Baal in Samaria and erected an altar for Baal in the temple.
See 1 Kings 16:32

God delivered Samaria from attack by Ben-Hadad, king of Aram.
See 1 Kings 20:1–21

Ahab and Jehoshaphat met in Samaria to plan an attack against Ramoth Gilead. Micaiah the prophet predicted failure. Ahab was killed in battle and carried back to Samaria for burial. His chariot was washed out by the pool of Samaria. Dogs licked up his blood, fulfilling Micaiah's prophecy.
See 1 Kings 22:1–40

Divided Kingdom

King Ahaziah of Israel fell through the lattice in the upper chamber of his palace in Samaria and died.
See 2 Kings 1:2–17

Divided Kingdom

The Arameans came to Dothan to capture Elisha, but God blinded them. Elisha led the army to Samaria, where their sight was restored.
See 2 Kings 6:8–23

The Arameans besieged Samaria and a great famine ensued. God delivered the city from the army and provided food for the inhabitants.
See 2 Kings 6:24–7:20

Ahab's seventy sons were slaughtered in Samaria, and their heads were sent to King Jehu in Jezreel.
See 2 Kings 10:1–7

The Assyrians besieged, captured, and destroyed the city of Samaria.
See 2 Kings 17:3–18

The prophet Hosea predicted God's judgment against Samaria for the people's idolatry.
See Hosea 7:1; 8:5–6; 10:5–7

The prophet Amos predicted God's judgment against Samaria for the people's social inequities.
See Amos 3:12; 4:1; 6:1

The prophet Micah predicted God's destruction of the city of Samaria, promising God would "pour her stones into the valley."
See Micah 1:1, 5–7

Babylonian Captivity   Gedaliah, the governor placed over Judah by the Babylonians after Jerusalem's fall, was murdered by Ishmael. The next day Ishmael also murdered seventy pilgrims from Shechem, Shiloh, and Samaria who were coming to Jerusalem to mourn the destruction of the temple.

See Jeremiah 41:5

Intertestamental Era   Alexander the Great conquered Samaria in 332 B.C. The city was completely destroyed in 108 B.C. by John Hyrcanus, who forced the inhabitants to convert to Judaism. Herod the Great later rebuilt the city and renamed it Sebaste in honor of the Roman emperor, Augustus Caesar. *(Sebaste* is the Greek translation of the Latin word *Augustus.)*

Remains of King Ahaz's palace at ancient Samaria.

Shechem

(SHEK uhm) Shechem, a key city in the hill country of Ephraim, played a central role in Israel's religious and civil history. Nestled between Mount Ebal and Mount Gerizim, the city watched a parade of historical giants, from Abraham to Jacob to Joshua to Jesus, pass through. After the destruction of Jerusalem in A.D. 70, a new city was established here for veterans of the Roman army. The city, named Neapolis ("new city"), gave its name to the present-day city of Nablus. For more information, see Ebal (Mount) and Gerizim (Mount).

Patriarchal Period

Abram's first stop in the Promised Land was Shechem.
See Genesis 12:6

Jacob's first stop when he returned to the Promised Land was Shechem.
See Genesis 33:18–19

Jacob's daughter, Dinah, was raped in Shechem. Her brothers avenged her by killing the men of the city.
See Genesis 34:1–31

Period of the Exodus

Moses commanded the Israelites to gather on Mount Ebal and Mount Gerizim to recite the blessings and cursings of the covenant. (Shechem is between Ebal and Gerizim.)
See Deuteronomy 27:4–13

Period of Conquest	Joshua gathered Israel on Mount Ebal and Mount Gerizim to recite the blessings and cursings of the covenant. *See Joshua 8:30–35*
Period of Conquest	Shechem, while near the border with Manasseh, was allotted to the tribe of Ephraim. *See Joshua 17:7; 1 Chronicles 7:28*
	Shechem was designated one of the six cities of refuge in the land of Israel. *See Joshua 20:1–9; 1 Chronicles 6:67*
	Joshua gathered all Israel to Shechem to renew their covenant with the Lord. *See Joshua 24:1–28*
	Israel buried the bones of Joseph in Shechem at the plot of ground purchased by Jacob. *See Joshua 24:32*
Period of the Judges	Abimelech, Gideon's son from a concubine who lived in Shechem (8:31), became Israel's first "king," although his rule was not sanctioned by the Lord. He ruled from Shechem, and he died in Shechem fighting his own people. *See Judges 9:1–57*
United Kingdom	King David affirmed God's ownership and control over portions of Israel, including Shechem. *See Psalms 60:6; 108:7*

Divided Kingdom

Rehoboam went to Shechem to be crowned king of all Israel. His harsh response to the northern tribes caused them to rebel against his authority.
See 1 Kings 12:1–24; 2 Chronicles 10:1–19

The first capital of the northern kingdom of Israel was established at Shechem.
See 1 Kings 12:25

Babylonian Captivity

Gedaliah, the governor placed over Judah by the Babylonians after Jerusalem's fall, was murdered by Ishmael. The next day Ishmael also murdered seventy pilgrims from Shechem, Shiloh, and Samaria who were coming to Jerusalem to mourn the destruction of the temple.
See Jeremiah 41:5

Life of Christ

Jesus met the Samaritan woman at Jacob's Well, near the ancient site of Shechem.
See John 4:1–42

Gateway to ancient Shechem.

Shiloh

Samaria

Jerusalem

(SHY loh) Shiloh became the first religious center for the tribes of Israel after they entered the land of Israel. The site's isolated, remote location gave it security; and its location in the central hills gave it accessibility to the entire nation.

Period of Conquest   Joshua gathered the Israelites to the tent of meeting at Shiloh. The remaining land allotments for the tribes were made at Shiloh.
See Joshua 18:1, 8–10

All Israel gathered at Shiloh to go to war against the tribes east of the Jordan River for setting up an altar. War was averted when the tribes explained the meaning of the altar.
See Joshua 22:10–12

Period of the Judges   The men from the tribe of Benjamin went to Shiloh to "capture" brides after their tribe was nearly destroyed in war. In describing the event, the writer gives an exact description of Shiloh's location "to the north of Bethel, and east of the road that goes from Bethel to Shechem, and to the south of Lebonah."
See Judges 21:15–22

Hannah prayed for a son at Shiloh. God answered her prayer, and she gave birth to Samuel.
See 1 Samuel 1:3–20

Samuel was dedicated to the Lord at Shiloh and remained at Shiloh to minister before

the Lord with Eli the priest. Eli's wicked sons displeased God at Shiloh.
See 1 Samuel 2:11–26

Period of the Judges

God appeared to Samuel at Shiloh and announced the destruction of Eli's family because of sin.
See 1 Samuel 3:1–21

Eli's sons took the ark from Shiloh, and it was captured by the Philistines. On hearing the news, Eli died. Although not mentioned directly in the Bible, it is likely that the various elements of the tabernacle were scattered throughout Israel at this time. Shiloh was abandoned by Israel or destroyed by the Philistines.
See 1 Samuel 4:1–22

The site where Israel erected the tabernacle at Shiloh.

Divided Kingdom   When King Jeroboam's son became ill, Jeroboam disguised his wife and sent her to Shiloh to visit the prophet Ahijah. Ahijah announced the child would die because of Jeroboam's sin.
See 1 Kings 14:1–4

The psalmist described how God "abandoned the tabernacle of Shiloh" because of Israel's idolatry.
See Psalm 78:60

Single Kingdom   The prophet Jeremiah used God's destruction of the tabernacle at Shiloh as an object lesson to judge the people of Jerusalem for idolatry.
See Jeremiah 7:12–14; 26:4–9

Babylonian Captivity   Gedaliah, the governor placed over Judah by the Babylonians after Jerusalem's fall, was murdered by Ishmael. The next day Ishmael also murdered seventy pilgrims from Shechem, Shiloh, and Samaria who were coming to Jerusalem to mourn the destruction of the temple.
See Jeremiah 41:5

Tabgha

(TAV gah) Tabgha is the site of several springs on the northwestern shore of the Sea of Galilee. The Arabic name comes from the Greek word heptapegon, which means "seven springs." These springs flow into the Sea of Galilee and provide a warm-water environment, especially in the winter, making the area one of the major fishing sites on the sea. This location has traditionally been identified as the site where Jesus performed the feeding of the five thousand (Mark 6:30–44). However, Luke 9:10 and John 6:1 seem to indicate that Jesus performed this miracle on the eastern side of the Sea of Galilee beyond the city of Bethsaida. While Tabgha is not the site where the feeding of the five thousand occurred, it is the likely spot where Jesus met with His disciples when they were fishing.

Life of Christ

Jesus called His disciples from their fishing boats to follow Him. They were now to become "fishers of men."
See Matthew 4:18–24; Mark 1:16–20; Luke 5:1–11

Following His resurrection, Jesus appeared to Peter and the other disciples along the shore of Galilee after they had experienced a long night of unproductive fishing. He instructed them to cast their nets on the right side of the boat, resulting in a large catch of fish. Jesus restored Peter from the shame of his prior denials and tested the depth of his love by asking three times, "Do you love me?" Here Jesus also commissioned Peter to "feed My sheep."
See John 21:1–24

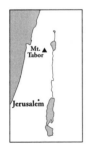

Tabor (Mount)

(TAY bour) Mount Tabor rises in splendid isolation from the floor of the Jezreel Valley. This single peak soars to a height of over 1,900 feet and towers over the International Highway at the point where the highway leaves the Jezreel Valley on its journey north toward the Sea of Galilee. Mount Tabor is the traditional site of the transfiguration, although Mount Hermon may be a better candidate.

Period of Conquest	Mount Tabor served as a boundary point between the tribes of Zebulun, Issachar, and Naphtali. *See Joshua 19:12, 22, 34*
	God allotted Mount Tabor as a special city for the Levites. *See 1 Chronicles 6:77*
Period of the Judges	Deborah and Barak gathered the army of Israel to Mount Tabor to fight against the army of Jabin, king of Hazor. Jabin's army was led by his general, Sisera. *See Judges 4:6, 12–16*
	Gideon killed the leaders of the Midianites because they had earlier slaughtered Gideon's brothers on Mount Tabor. *See Judges 8:18–21*
Single Kingdom	The psalmist used the heights of Mount Tabor and Mount Hermon to describe God's exalted creation. *See Psalm 89:12*

Single Kingdom

The prophet Jeremiah compared the grandeur of Nebuchadnezzar to the exalted height of Mount Tabor or Mount Carmel. *See Jeremiah 46:18*

Life of Christ

Mount Tabor is the traditional site of the "Mount of Transfiguration" because of its height. *See Matthew 17:1–9; Mark 9:2–9; Luke 9:28–37*

Mt. Tabor, located a few miles southeast of Nazareth.

Tiberias

(ty BIHR ih uhs) The city of Tiberias was founded by Herod Antipas in A.D. 17–20 and was named after Tiberias Caesar, the emperor of Rome (A.D. 14–37). Tiberias was the emperor when Jesus began His public ministry (Luke 3:1). This city also gave its name to the Sea of Tiberias (i.e., the Sea of Galilee). There is no record that Jesus visited Tiberias. The area was known for its therapeutic hot springs, and this may explain in part why large numbers of sick people came to Jesus for healing when He was in the area.

Life of Christ

Jesus predicted judgment for several towns around the Sea of Galilee—Korazin, Bethsaida, and Capernaum—and they are gone. He did not pronounce judgment on Tiberias, and it remains.
See Matthew 11:20–24

Jesus ministered on the Sea of Tiberias, and curious residents sailed their boats from Tiberias to witness His miracles.
See John 6:1; 21:1

Looking down at the Sea of Galilee from top of modern Tiberias.

Section Three

The Land of Jordan

Amman/Ammon/ Ammonites

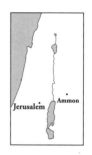

The Ammonites descended from a son born to Lot and his youngest daughter following the destruction of Sodom and Gomorrah (Gen. 19:30–38). Because the Ammonites descended from Lot (Abraham's nephew), they were considered a "related" nation to Israel. "And when you come opposite the sons of Ammon, do not harass them nor provoke them, for I will not give you any of the land of the sons of Ammon as a possession, because I have given it to the sons of Lot as a possession" (Deut. 2:19). The Ammonites occupied the tableland east of the Jordan Valley that stretched into the Arabian desert. Their northern boundary extended to the Jabbok River, while their southern boundary was the Arnon River. The capital of the Ammonites was Rabbah (sometimes called Rabbath-ammon). The national god of the Ammonites was Molech.

By New Testament times, the city of Rabbah had become the south-ernmost city in the league of cities called the Decapolis. Its name had been changed to Philadelphia (not to be confused with the city of Philadelphia in Asia Minor named in the Book of Revelation). Today, ancient Rabbah is the modern city of Amman, Jordan, the capital of the Hashemite Kingdom of Jordan.

Patriarchal Period	Lot's younger daughter got her father drunk and had sexual relations with him. The child born of that union was named Ben-Ammi ("son of my father"), and the Ammonites descended from him. *See Genesis 19:30–38*
Period of the Exodus	God prohibited Israel from taking the land of the Ammonites. *See Deuteronomy 2:19–21, 37*
Period of the Judges	The Ammonites united with Eglon, king of Moab, to oppress Israel and control the city of Jericho. *See Judges 3:13*
	The Ammonites oppressed Israel until Jephthah rose as a judge to deliver the Israelites from them. *See Judges 10–11*
United Kingdom	Saul's first act as king was to rescue the people of Jabesh Gilead from an Ammonite attack. *See 1 Samuel 11*
	The Ammonites humiliated a delegation sent by King David and brought about war with Israel. Joab defeated the Ammonites in battle near Medeba. *See 2 Samuel 10; cp. 1 Chronicles 19:7*
	Joab and the men of Israel fought the Ammonites and besieged their capital of Rabbah. David remained in Jerusalem and committed adultery with Bathsheba. Uriah, Bathsheba's husband, was killed in the siege of Rabbah. *See 2 Samuel 11*

Divided Kingdom

The Ammonites, Moabites, and Edomites united and crossed the Dead Sea at the tongue of land called the Lisan to attack Judah. Jehoshaphat led the Israelites into the wilderness, only to discover that God had already intervened and caused the allies to fight among themselves and kill one another.
See 2 Chronicles 20

King Uzziah forced the Ammonites to pay tribute to him.
See 2 Chronicles 26:8

Following Uzziah's death, King Jotham attacked and defeated the Ammonites, forcing them to continue paying tribute to Judah.
See 2 Chronicles 27:5

God condemned the Ammonites for attacking the Israelite land of Gilead, east of the Sea of Galilee.
See Amos 1:13–15

Babylonian Captivity

After Jerusalem's fall to the Babylonians, the king of Ammon sent Ishmael to assassinate Gedaliah, the governor of Judah appointed by the Babylonians. After the assassination, Ishmael fled to Ammon.
See Jeremiah 40:13–14; 41:2–15

Jeremiah predicted the imminent destruction of "Rabbah of the Ammonites." But he also predicted the Ammonites' eventual restoration.
See Jeremiah 49:1–6

Babylonian Captivity

When Nebuchadnezzar brought his army from Babylon, he had to decide whether to attack first Rabbah of the Ammonites or Jerusalem. Ezekiel prophesied God would direct Nebuchadnezzar to Jerusalem.
See Ezekiel 21:18–27

Ezekiel predicted the imminent destruction of the Ammonites because they rejoiced when the Babylonians destroyed Jerusalem.
See Ezekiel 25:1–7

Daniel predicted that Edom, Moab, and Ammon would not fall into the hands of the final world ruler who would invade Israel just before the coming of Israel's Messiah.
See Daniel 11:41

Zephaniah promised that God would judge the people of Ammon for their taunts against Jerusalem.
See Zephaniah 2:8–9

Restoration

The Ammonites harassed the Jews who returned from captivity, threatened the security of those who were rebuilding Jerusalem, and tried to corrupt the remnant through intermarriage.
See Ezra 9:1; Nehemiah 4:7; 13:23

Arnon River

The Arnon River runs from east to west and drains into the Dead Sea approximately half way down its eastern side. From antiquity it has served as a natural barrier and border.

Period of the Exodus

"The Arnon is the border of Moab, between Moab and the Amorites."
See Numbers 21:13

King Balak of Moab went to meet the prophet Balaam at a "Moabite town on the Arnon border."
See Numbers 22:36

Israel captured all the land of Sihon, king of the Amorites, which began at Aroer "on the rim of the Arnon Gorge."
See Deuteronomy 2:24–37; also see Joshua 12:1–2

The territory of the Amorites, captured by Israel, extended from the Arnon Gorge north to Mount Hermon.
See Deuteronomy 3:8

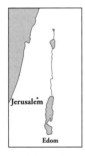

Jerusalem

Edom

Edom/Edomites

The Edomites were the descendants of Jacob's twin brother, Esau (Gen. 25:21–26; 36:9). The name Edom comes from a word meaning "red," and it described Esau's physical characteristics at birth (Gen. 25:25). It also became his nickname because of his fondness for red lentil stew, the "red stuff" for which he bartered away his birthright (Gen. 25:30–31). Finally, the name is an apt description of the land occupied by the Edomites with its red sandstone rock.

Because the Edomites descended from Esau (Jacob's brother), they were considered a "brother" nation to Israel. Moses commanded Israel, "Do not abhor an Edomite, for he is your brother" (Deut. 23:7).

The northern border of the land of Edom was the Wadi Zered that flows from east to west and joins the Arabah at the southeastern tip of the Dead Sea. The land of the Edomites extended south to the Red Sea, or the Gulf of Aqaba.

Patriarchal Period	Esau left the land of Canaan and settled in the land of Seir, later known as Edom. *See Genesis 32:3; 36:6–8*
Period of the Exodus	The Edomites refused to let Israel pass through their land as the Israelites made their way up the east side of the Dead Sea. Israel had asked for permission to travel on the "King's Highway" (the main north-south road from Damascus to the Gulf of Aqaba) where it passed through Edom. *See Numbers 20:14–21*

Period of the Exodus	The Desert of Zin, along the southeastern border of the tribe of Judah, was the boundary between Israel and Edom. *See Numbers 34:3; cp. Joshua 15:1*
United Kingdom	Doeg the Edomite spotted David when he fled from Saul to the priests of Nob to retrieve Goliath's sword. Doeg later reported the event to Saul and personally killed eighty-five priests at the order of Saul. *See 1 Samuel 21:7; cp. 1 Samuel 22:9–19*
	David destroyed an Edomite army and conquered the land of Edom. (NOTE: Second Samuel 8:13 should read "Edomites" rather than "Arameans.") *See 2 Samuel 8:13–14;* *cp. 1 Chronicles 18:12–13*
	Solomon built a fleet of ships at Ezion Geber near Elath "in Edom, on the shore of the Red Sea." *See 1 Kings 9:26; cp. 2 Chronicles 8:17*
	God raised up Hadad the Edomite as an adversary to judge King Solomon for his unfaithfulness. *See 1 Kings 11:14*
Divided Kingdom	The kings of Judah, Israel, and Edom led their armies through the desert of Edom in a surprise attack against the King of Moab. *See 2 Kings 3:4–27*

Divided Kingdom

The Edomites rebelled against Judah's control during the reign of Jehoram.
See 2 Kings 8:20–22;
cp. 2 Chronicles 21:8–10

King Amaziah of Judah defeated ten thousand Edomites in a major battle and captured the city of Sela.
See 2 Kings 14:7

The king of Aram captured Elath from Judah and drove out the people of Judah. The Edomites moved back to populate the city.
See 2 Kings 16:6

The Ammonites, Moabites, and Edomites united and crossed the Dead Sea at the Lisan to attack Judah. Jehoshaphat led the Israelites into the wilderness, only to discover that God had already intervened and caused the allies to fight among themselves and kill one another.
See 2 Chronicles 20

The Edomites attacked Judah during the reign of Ahaz.
See 2 Chronicles 28:17

Isaiah prophesied a day when God's people would triumph over Edom, Moab, and Ammon.
See Isaiah 11:14

Divided Kingdom

In picturing God's final judgment on the earth as He intervened to judge sin and restore His people Israel, Isaiah recorded that God's sword "descends in judgment on Edom" (v. 5).
See Isaiah 34:1–11

Isaiah pictured God coming from Edom with His robe stained in the blood of His enemies.
See Isaiah 63:1–3

God would make Edom a desolate waste because of their violence against the people of Judah.
See Joel 3:19

God condemned Edom for pursuing "his brother [Judah] with a sword, stifling all compassion."
See Amos 1:11–12

The prophet Obadiah described God's judgment on the prideful people of Edom.
See the Book of Obadiah

Babylonian Captivity

The psalmist asked God to judge the Edomites for their boastful taunting over Jerusalem when it fell to the Babylonians.
See Psalm 137:7

Jeremiah described God's judgment against Edom.
See Jeremiah 49:7–22

Edom rejoiced over the fall of Jerusalem, but God promised to punish Edom for its sin.
See Lamentations 4:21–22

Babylonian Captivity

God vowed to destroy Edom because the Edomites had taken revenge on the people of Judah.
See Ezekiel 25:12–14

God vowed to destroy Edom because they tried to take by force the land that God had promised to His people Israel.
See Ezekiel 35:1–15

Daniel predicted that Edom, Moab, and Ammon would not fall into the hands of the final world ruler who would invade Israel just before the coming of Israel's Messiah.
See Daniel 11:41

Restoration

God vowed the Edomites would not be allowed to rise again. Instead, they would remain under the wrath of the Lord.
See Malachi 1:4

The mountainous landscape of the land of Edom.

Jabbok River

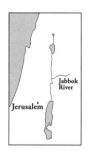

The Jabbok River runs from east to west and drains into the Jordan River approximately halfway between the Sea of Galilee and the Dead Sea. From antiquity, it has served as a natural barrier and border dividing Upper Gilead from Lower Gilead.

Patriarchal Period

Jacob wrestled with God at Peniel by the Jabbok River when he returned to the Promised Land after his years in Paddan Aram. God renamed Jacob and called him "Israel."
See Genesis 32

Period of Conquest

The Jabbok River was the boundary between the Israelites on the east of the Jordan River and the Ammonites.
See Deuteronomy 3:16

Period of the Judges
The Ammonites had lost some of their land to the Amorites before the time of the Exodus. Their desire to retake that land from the Israelites (who had captured it from Sihon, king of the Amorites) led to Ammon's defeat at the hands of Jephthah and the Israelites.
See Judges 11:13–33

Panoramic view of the Jabbok River.

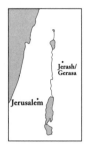

Jerash/
Gerasa

Jerusalem

Jerash/Gerasa

The modern city of Jerash in Jordan preserves the name of the ancient city of Gerasa, one of the most important cities in the region of the Decapolis. The city is located about twenty-five miles north of Amman, Jordan, and about forty miles southeast of the Sea of Galilee. Jerash has some of the best preserved Roman ruins in the Middle East.

The only possible reference to Gerasa in the New Testament occurs in the account of Jesus casting the demons into the herd of swine. Matthew 8:28–34 records the exact location where the miracle occurred. Matthew, writing to a Jewish audience more familiar with the geographical details of the land, could record the specific village along the shore of the Sea of Galilee. However, Mark (writing to a Roman audience) and Luke (writing to a Greek audience) recorded the nearest large city that would be familiar to their readers. While there is a textual problem that divides scholars, the two possible cities named by Mark and Luke are Gadara (a smaller city six miles from the Sea of Galilee) or Gerasa (the larger city forty miles from the Sea of Galilee). If Gerasa is the correct textual reading, then Mark and Luke were pointing to the region dominated by the city called Gerasa (modern Jerash).

Life of Christ

Jesus and His disciples crossed the Sea of Galilee "to the region of the Gerasenes [i.e., Gerasa]."
See Mark 5:1

Jesus and His disciples "sailed to the region of the Gerasenes [i.e., Gerasa], which is across the lake from Galilee."
See Luke 8:26

Moab/Moabites

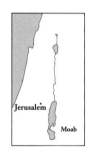

Jerusalem

Moab

The Moabites descended from a son born to Lot and his oldest daughter following the destruction of Sodom and Gomorrah (Gen. 19:30–38). Because the Moabites descended from Lot (Abraham's nephew), they were considered a "related" nation to Israel. "Do not harass the Moabites or provoke them to war, for I will not give you any part of their land. I have given Ar to the descendants of Lot as a possession" (Deut. 2:9). The Moabites occupied the tableland east of the Dead Sea. Their northern boundary extended to the Arnon River, and their southern boundary extended to the Zered River. However, in times of strength their territory did expand northward beyond the Arnon River. Thus, the place where Israel crossed the Jordan into the Promised Land was called the "plains of Moab." The national god of the Moabites was Chemosh.

Patriarchal Period	Lot's oldest daughter got her father drunk and had sexual relations with him. The child born of that union was named Moab, and the Moabites descended from him. *See Genesis 19:30–38*
Period of the Exodus	Israel skirted past Moab on its journey northward along the eastern side of the Dead Sea. *See Numbers 21:11–13; cp. Judges 11:17–18*
	Balak, king of Moab, summoned the prophet Balaam to curse the nation of Israel. *See Numbers 22–24*
	Although Balaam was unable to curse Israel outright, he evidently urged the Moabite women to entice the men of Israel into idolatry. *See Numbers 25; cp. Revelation 2:14*

Period of the Exodus	God prohibited Israel from taking the land of the Moabites. *See Deuteronomy 2:9–18*
Period of the Judges	Eglon, king of Moab, oppressed Israel for eighteen years and controlled the city of Jericho until he was defeated by the judge, Ehud. *See Judges 3:12–30*
	Elimelech, Naomi, and their two sons fled to Moab to escape a famine in Bethlehem. The husband and two sons died. Naomi returned to Bethlehem accompanied by one of her daughters-in-law, Ruth the Moabitess. Ruth married Boaz, and from their line came King David (Ruth 4:22) and Jesus (Matt. 1:5, 16). *See the Book of Ruth*
United Kingdom	King Saul conducted military campaigns against Moab. *See 1 Samuel 14:47*
	David, while a fugitive from Saul, took his parents to live in Moab. *See 1 Samuel 22:3–4*
	David conquered the Moabites and made them his subjects. *See 2 Samuel 8:2; cp. 1 Chronicles 18:2*

Divided Kingdom

After King Ahab's death, Moab rebelled against the northern kingdom of Israel.
See 2 Kings 1:1

The kings of Israel, Judah, and Edom attacked and defeated the Moabites.
See 2 Kings 3

The Ammonites, Moabites, and Edomites united together and crossed the Dead Sea at the Lisan to attack Judah. Jehoshaphat led the Israelites into the wilderness, only to discover that God had already intervened and caused the allies to fight among themselves and kill one another.
See 2 Chronicles 20

Isaiah prophesied a day when God's people would triumph over Edom, Moab, and Ammon.
See Isaiah 11:14

Isaiah presented God's oracle of judgment against the people of Moab because of their excessive pride.
See Isaiah 15–16

Amos announced God's judgment on the people of Moab because of their callous disregard even for the dead.
See Amos 2:1–3

Babylonian Captivity Jeremiah presented God's prophecy of destruction against the people of Moab for their prideful self-reliance and their gloating over Judah's destruction.
See Jeremiah 48

Ezekiel predicted Moab's destruction because of the nation's refusal to acknowledge God's special place for Israel.
See Ezekiel 25:8–11

Daniel predicted that Edom, Moab, and Ammon would not fall into the hands of the final world ruler who would invade Israel just before the coming of Israel's Messiah.
See Daniel 11:41

Zephaniah promised God would judge the people of Moab because of their prideful insults over Judah's destruction.
See Zephaniah 2:8–10

Restoration Nehemiah rebuked the people of Judah for mixed marriages, including marriages to women of Moab.
See Nehemiah 13:23–27

Nabateans

The Nabateans were Semitic nomads who developed and controlled the land caravan routes in the Middle East. Their early history is obscure, but by the fourth century B.C. they had taken control of Petra from the Edomites, forcing the remaining Edomite population to migrate westward into the Negev and wilderness area in southern Judea.

Although the Nabateans began as nomadic traders, they eventually settled into cities that sat strategically along the main trade routes. Several such cities are in Israel (Mamphsis, Avdat/Oboda), but the city known best is Petra. The beautiful buildings carved into the hillside were constructed by the Nabateans and, later, by the Romans who captured the city in A.D. 106.

The Nabateans' sudden, swift conquest of the land of Edom and expulsion of the Edomites seems to confirm Obadiah's prophecy against Edom: "All your allies will force you to the border; your friends will deceive and overpower you; those who eat your bread will set a trap for you" (Obad. 7). The Edomites welcomed the caravans of the Nabateans, and the wealth they brought, into their land . . .

only to discover their "allies" would later become their conquerors.

More excavations from the Nabatean time period at the ancient city of Mamphsis.

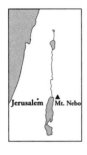

Jerusalem ▲ Mt. Nebo

Nebo (Mount)

Mount Nebo, also identified with Pisgah, was located northeast of the Dead Sea overlooking the Jordan Valley opposite Jericho. A town with the same name was nearby. It is unclear whether the town was named for the mountain or the mountain for the town.

Period of the Exodus

The king of Moab took Balaam the prophet to "the top of Pisgah" in an effort to get Balaam to curse Israel.
See Numbers 23:13–14

The tribe of Reuben received the city of Nebo as part of their tribal inheritance.
See Numbers 32:3, 38

God allowed Moses to view the Promised Land from "Mount Nebo in Moab, across from Jericho." The specific mountain on which Moses stood was called "the top of Pisgah."
See Deuteronomy 32:49; 34:1

Divided Kingdom

Isaiah predicted the inhabitants of Nebo and Medeba would weep at the time of their coming destruction.
See Isaiah 15:2

Single Kingdom

Jeremiah predicted the destruction of Nebo and the other cities located on the "plateau."
See Jeremiah 48:1, 21–22

Petra

Petra, the rose-red capital of the Nabateans, was originally a city of the Edomites (2 Kings 14:7). Some believe the Old Testament city of Sela (from the Hebrew word meaning "jagged cliff, craggy rock") is the same as the Nabatean city of Petra (from the Greek word meaning "the rock"). However, it seems best not to equate the two cities. The city of Petra is located in a semi-landlocked valley on the eastern side of the Arabah, approximately fifty miles south of the Dead Sea.

The normal entrance into the city of Petra is through the Siq ("cleft"), a winding fissure in the eastern ridge. At the end of the Siq, the path opens up to a canyon . . . and a spectacular view of a temple carved into the face of the rock.

Some Bible teachers believe the people of Israel will flee to Petra during the period of tribulation immediately preceding the return of Jesus Christ to earth to set up His kingdom. These teachers cite several passages of Scripture to support this view. Those Scriptures are listed below.

Divided Kingdom
"All the stars of the heavens will be dissolved and the sky rolled up like a scroll; all the starry host will fall . . . . My sword has drunk its fill in the heavens; see, it descends in judgment on Edom . . . . For the LORD has a sacrifice in Bozrah and a great slaughter in Edom."
See Isaiah 34:4–6

"Who is this coming from Edom, from Bozrah, with his garments stained crimson? Who is this, robed in splendor, striding forward in the greatness of his strength?"
See Isaiah 63:1

Life of Christ

"So when you see standing in the holy place 'the abomination that causes desolation,' spoken of through the prophet Daniel—let the reader understand—then let those who are in Judea flee to the mountains."
See Matthew 24:15–16

Apostolic Age

"The woman [Israel] fled into the desert to a place prepared for her by God, where she might be taken care of for 1,260 days."
See Revelation 12:6

Khazneh Far'un, *the "treasury of the Pharoah," at Petra.*

Wadi Zered

Wadi Zered

The Wadi Zered runs from southeast to northwest and drains into the southern edge of the Dead Sea. From antiquity, it has served as a natural barrier and border. It was the traditional border between Moab and Edom.

Period of the Exodus   Israel camped by the Wadi Zered on their journey around the eastern side of the Dead Sea.
See Numbers 21:12,
cf. Deuteronomy 2:13–14

Divided Kingdom   The valley that filled with water when Israel, Judah, and Edom attacked Moab was probably the Wadi Zered on Moab's border.
See 2 Kings 3:16–27

The "brook of the Arabim" over which Moab's wealth would be carried is probably the Wadi Zered.
See Isaiah 15:7

The "valley of the Arabah" named by Amos was probably the Wadi Zered, and it marked the southernmost boundary controlled by the King of Israel.
See Amos 6:14

Section Four

The Lands of the Aegean

Athens

Athens, the most important city in ancient Greece, was famous for its culture, learning, and great philosophers like Plato and Aristotle. The city was also renowned for its temples, statues, and monuments. After the Romans conquered Greece, Athens became a *civitas foederata* (a city linked to Rome by treaty), entirely independent of the governor of Achaia and paying no taxes to Rome. Although the Athenians were religious and eager to discuss religion, their spiritual level was not exceptionally high.

Apostolic Age

Paul came to Athens on his second missionary journey and preached to the philosophers at the Areopagus (Mars Hill).
See Acts 17:15–34

While in Athens, Paul sent Timothy back to Thessalonica to see how the new church there was doing since he had been forced to leave early. Before Timothy could return with news from Thessalonica, Paul left Athens for Corinth.
See 1 Thessalonians 3:1–6

Corinth

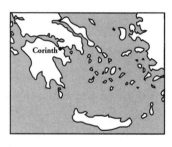

Corinth was situated at the western end of the narrow isthmus linking central Greece and the Peloponnesian peninsula. Because of its position, Corinth controlled the trade route between northern Greece and the Peloponnesian peninsula as well as the route across the isthmus. Ships would unload cargo and transport it overland for five miles between the eastern port at Cenchrea and the western port at Lechaeum to avoid the hazardous voyage around the peninsula. The rocky mountain jutting up south of the city, called the Acrocorinth, dominated the landscape around Corinth. In ancient times, a temple to Aphrodite, goddess of love, stood on its crest with one thousand prostitutes serving those who came to "worship." The one thousand prostitutes plus the transient population gave Corinth the reputation of an immoral city. The degree to which Corinth was given over to vice is seen in the coining of the words *korinthiázomi* (lit., "to Corinthianize") which meant "to practice immorality" and *korinthia kórē* (lit., "Corinthian girl") which meant "prostitute."

Apostolic Age	On his second missionary journey, Paul came to Corinth after leaving Athens. Paul teamed up for the first time with Aquila and Priscilla in Corinth, and he remained in the city for eighteen months, planting the church. The Jews opposed Paul and brought him before the judgment seat of Gallio, proconsul of Achaia. *See Acts 18:1–18*

Paul wrote the letter of 1 Corinthians from Ephesus while on his third missionary journey. Paul wrote to correct a number of problems that had arisen in the Corinthian church after his departure. The letter was |

written in advance of a planned trip to Corinth by Paul.
See 1 Corinthians 16:5–9

Apostolic Age

Paul made a second, unrecorded, visit to Corinth, possibly while he was still at Ephesus (2 Cor. 2:1; 12:14; 13:1–2). The exact nature of the visit is uncertain, but it was not anticipated by Paul when he wrote 1 Corinthians (cp. 1 Cor. 16:5–7). These veiled references imply it was an emergency trip made in haste, possibly to correct some severe problems that had arisen in Corinth.

Paul wrote the letter of 2 Corinthians from Macedonia (possibly Philippi) when he received good news from Titus about the repentance in the church at Corinth. Paul was coming to Corinth to complete the collection being made for the saints in Jerusalem (2 Cor. 9:1–5). This was to be his third trip to Corinth.
See 2 Corinthians 12:14; 13:1–2.

Paul went to Greece to complete the collection for the saints and spent three months in Greece (some of which, no doubt, was spent in Corinth).
See Acts 20:2–3

Crete

The island of Crete is a large island in the Mediterranean Sea that forms the southern boundary of the Aegean Sea. The island is 156 miles long and varies in width from 8 to 35 miles. The mountains in the interior reach a height of 8,000 feet. These drop sharply into the Mediterranean Sea along the southern coast. As a result, most of Crete's good harbors are on the northern side. During the Bronze Age (ca. 2000–1200 B.C.), the Minoan civilization flourished on Crete. The capital was at Knossos, and extensive ruins of the Minoan palace at Knossos can still be seen. In the Old Testament, the island of Crete is referred to as Caphtor; and the people who came from Crete are called "Caphtorim," "Caphtorites," "Cherethites," and "Kerethites." They were either identical to, or closely related to, the Philistines. The inhabitants of Crete were not known for their strong moral integrity. In Greek literature, "to Cretanize" meant "to lie."

Period of the Exodus Moses used the inhabitants of Crete (who, possibly, became the Philistines) as an example of those who drove out other inhabitants and settled in their land: "And as for the Avvites who lived in villages as far as Gaza, the Caphtorites coming out from Caphtor destroyed them and settled in their place." *See Deuteronomy 2:23*

United Kingdom The land of the Kerethites was raided by the same group who destroyed David's city of Ziklag. The land of the Kerethites was the southern Gaza strip area and was also considered the land of the Philistines. *See 1 Samuel 30:1; cp. Genesis 26:1; 1 Samuel 6:1*

United Kingdom

Part of David's personal contingent of soldiers and bodyguards included "Kerethites and Pelethites." These were a special military contingent of mercenary soldiers who had their own leader: "Joab was over Israel's entire army; Benaiah son of Jehoiada was over the Kerethites and Pelethites" (2 Sam. 20:23).

See 2 Samuel 8:18; 15:18; 20:7, 23

Divided Kingdom

Amos explained the origin of the Philistines: "Did I [the LORD] not bring Israel up from Egypt, the Philistines from Caphtor and the Arameans from Kir?"

See Amos 9:7

Single Kingdom

Ezekiel predicted God's destruction of the Philistines/Kerethites because of their persecution of Israel: "I am about to stretch out my hand against the Philistines, and I will cut off the Kerethites and destroy those remaining along the coast."

See Ezekiel 25:16

After naming the cities of Gaza, Ashkelon, Ashdod, and Ekron—four of the five cities that were part of the land of the Philistines—Zephaniah predicted God's destruction of the Philistines/Kerethite: "Woe to you who live by the sea, O Kerethite people; the word of the LORD is against you, O Canaan, land of the Philistines."

See Zephaniah 2:5

Apostolic Age

Jews from Crete were present in Jerusalem on the Day of Pentecost.
See Acts 2:11

On his way to Rome as a prisoner, Paul's ship "sailed to the lee of Crete, opposite Salmone." The Book of Acts describes the ship's journey along the southern coast to a place called Fair Havens, near the town of Lasea. Since the harbor was unsuitable to winter in, the majority decided to sail on, hoping to reach Phoenix (on southwestern Crete) and winter there: "Before very long, a wind of hurricane force, called the 'northeaster,' swept down from the island. The ship was caught by the storm and could not head into the wind."
See Acts 27:7–15, 21

After his first imprisonment, Paul evidently returned to Crete to continue his missionary activity. Paul journeyed on but left Titus in Crete to finish the work he had begun. Paul quoted Epimenides (a sixth-century B.C. native of Knossos, Crete) who wrote that "Cretans are always liars, evil brutes, lazy gluttons." Sadly, Paul noted, "This testimony is true."
See Titus 1:5, 12–13

Ephesus

Ephesus was an important seaport city in the Roman province of Asia. The city was also located at the intersection of two major overland routes—the coastal road that ran north through Smyrna and Pergamum to Troas, and the road that ran west to Colossae, Laodicea, and the interior of Asia Minor. This strategic location made Ephesus a major commercial and religious center. The temple of Artemis (Diana) was known throughout the Mediterranean area, and thousands of pilgrims flocked to Ephesus during the festivals of Artemis. Heroditus identified this temple as one of the seven wonders of the ancient world.

Inside the temple was a statue of Artemis (Diana) that was at least partially fashioned from a meteorite. This explains the statement of the city clerk in Ephesus in Acts 19:35: "Men of Ephesus, doesn't all the world know that the city of Ephesus is the guardian of the temple of the great Artemis and of her image, which fell from heaven?" During the time of the New Testament, the city likely had a population in excess of two hundred fifty thousand. The city theater could seat twenty-five thousand.

Apostolic Age	Paul stopped briefly in Ephesus on his return to Jerusalem at the end of his second missionary journey. Paul left Priscilla and Aquila behind in Ephesus while he returned to Jerusalem. Later, Priscilla and Aquila discipled Apollos in Ephesus before Apollos went on to Achaia (and Corinth). *See Acts 18:19–28*

Apostolic Age

Paul went to Ephesus on his third missionary journey and stayed there for nearly three years. He spoke in the Jewish synagogue for three months and then had daily discussions in the lecture hall of Tyrannus. Paul's time in Ephesus ended following a riot incited by the silversmiths.
See Acts 19:1–20:1

On his return to Jerusalem at the end of his third missionary journey, Paul decided against stopping in Ephesus. But while in Miletus he called for the elders of the church at Ephesus and warned them against false teachers who would try to slip in among them.
See Acts 20:17–38

While imprisoned for the first time in Rome, Paul wrote his letter to the Ephesians. The date of this letter is approximately A.D. 60. The letter was probably intended both for the church at Ephesus and for the churches in the surrounding area.
See the Book of Ephesians

After Paul's release from his first Roman imprisonment, he evidently returned to Ephesus about A.D. 65–66 as part of his further travels. Paul's earlier warning to the elders concerning false teachers must have come true, and Paul left Timothy in Ephesus to "command certain men not to teach false doctrines any longer" (1 Tim. 1:3). Shortly after leaving Ephesus and heading to Nicopolis, Paul was arrested, taken to Rome, tried, and beheaded.
See 1 Timothy 1:3

Apostolic Age

Tradition says the apostle John settled in Ephesus and had a profound impact on the city. During the reign of Domitian, John was exiled from Ephesus to the Island of Patmos. It was there that he wrote the Book of Revelation about A.D. 95. The first of the seven letters to the churches written in the Book of Revelation was addressed to the church at Ephesus.

See Revelation 2:1–7

A part of the Roman Harbor Baths and Gymnasium complex excavated at ancient Ephesus.

MODERN POLITICAL DIVISIONS OF ANCIENT PALESTINE

- • City
- • City (modern name)
- ▲ Mountain peak
- —— Present day International boundaries
- ---- Disputed boundaries

MEDITERRANEAN SEA

33°N

0 10 20 30 40 50 Miles
0 10 20 30 40 50 Kilometers

LEBANON

Sidon

Litani River

Metulla

Qiryat Shemona

Nahariyya

Acco

Zefat

Haifa

Tiberias

Megiddo

Afula

Janin

Hadera

Netanya

Nablus

Shechem

Tel Aviv

WEST BANK

Ramallah

Jericho

Rehovot

Jerusalem

Bethlehem

Hebron

Gaza

GAZA STRIP

En-gedi

Beersheba

Al-Arish

W. al-Arish

Dimona

DEAD SEA

Kerak

EGYPT

Mizpe Ramon

Damascus

Abana River

Mt. Hermon

Pharpar River

SYRIA

GOLAN HEIGHTS

Sea of Galilee

Yarmuk River

Irbid

Beth-shan

Jabbok River

Amman

JORDAN

Madaba

Arnon River

Zered River

36°E

33°N

32°N

32°N

31°N

31°N

34°E

35°E

Aerial view of Jerusalem.

The original city of Jerusalem looking southwest across the Kidron Valley from the Mount of Olives.

The bell tower of the Church of the Dormition, adjacent to the traditional upper room, in Jerusalem.

Stephen's (or Lion's) Gate at Jerusalem.

The Damascus Gate at Jerusalem as seen from outside the old city walls.

Model of Herod's temple showing view into the inner court.

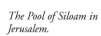

The Pool of Siloam in Jerusalem.

A closeup view of the Dome of the Rock built on the site of Solomon's Temple.

Notes containing prayer requests are still placed between the massive stones of the Western Wall.

Modern orthodox Jews praying at the Western Wall of the Temple Mount in Jerusalem.

View of Bethlehem from tower of Church of the Nativity.

One of the so-called "Pools of Solomon" just south of Bethlehem.

173

The Mount of Temptation as seen from the top of Old Testament Jericho.

A Christian monastery on the Mount of Temptation marks the traditional site of Jesus' temptation.

Cliffs of Mount Arbel with the Sea of Galilee in the background.

Boat at anchor on the Sea of Galilee.

Church of the Beatitudes on the traditional site of the Sermon on the Mount by the Sea of Galilee.

The Sea of Galilee as viewed from the northwest.

Synagogue at Capernaum.

The traditional site of the tomb of Lazarus in Bethany.

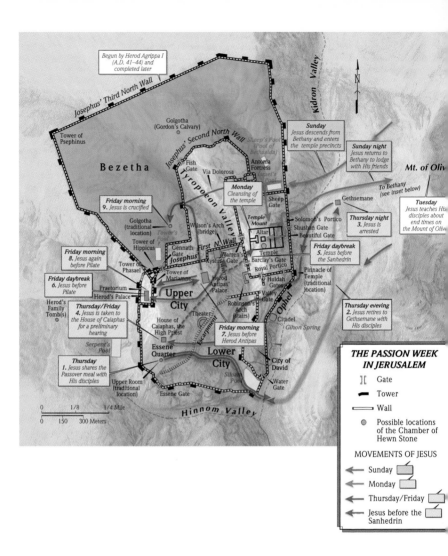

Begun by Herod Agrippa I
(A.D. 41–44) and
completed later

Josephus' Third North Wall

Golgotha
(Gordon's Calvary)

Tower of
Psephinus

Bezetha

Fish
Gate

Via Dolorosa

Sunday
Jesus descends from
Bethany and enters
the temple precincts

Sunday night
Jesus returns to
Bethany to lodge
with His friends

Sheep's Pool
(Pool of
Bethesda)

Antonia
Fortress

Israel's

Mt. of Oliv

To Bethany
(see inset below)

Gethsemane

Josephus' Second North Wall

Tyropoeon Valley

Friday morning
9. Jesus is crucified

Golgotha
(traditional
location)

Tower's
Pool

Wilson's Arch
(bridge)

Gennath
Gate

Tower of
Hippicus

Friday morning
8. Jesus again
before Pilate

Tower of
Phasael

Friday daybreak
6. Jesus before
Pilate

Praetorium

Herod's Palace

Herod's
Family
Tomb(s)

Thursday/Friday
4. Jesus is taken to
the House of Caiaphas
for a preliminary
hearing

Serpent's
Pool

Thursday
1. Jesus shares the
Passover meal with
His disciples

Essene
Quarter

Monday
Cleansing of
the temple

Temple
Mount

Altar

First N. Wall

Warren's
Gate

Xystus

Barclay's Gate

Royal Portico

Temple

Sheep
Gate

Solomon's Portico

Shushan Gate

Beautiful Gate

Thursday night
3. Jesus is
arrested

Friday daybreak
5. Jesus before
the Sanhedrin

Tuesday
Jesus teaches His
disciples about
end times on
the Mount of Oliv

Josephus'

Tower of
Mariamne

Herod
Antipas'
Palace

Upper
City

Theater

Robinson's
Arch
(stairs)

Escarpment

House of
Caiaphas, the
High Priest

Lower
City

Friday morning
7. Jesus before
Herod Antipas

Huldah
Gates

Valley
Gate

Citadel

Gihon Spring

Pinnacle of
Temple
(traditional
location)

Ophel

Thursday evening
2. Jesus retires to
Gethsemane with
His disciples

City of
David

Siloam
Pool

Water
Gate

Upper Room
(traditional
location)

Essene Gate

0   1/8   1/4 Mile
0   150   300 Meters

Hinnom Valley

Kidron Valley

N

**THE PASSION WEEK
IN JERUSALEM**

][Gate

⬅   Tower

⟺   Wall

⦿   Possible locations
of the Chamber of
Hewn Stone

MOVEMENTS OF JESUS

⬅   Sunday

⬅   Monday

⬅   Thursday/Friday

⬅   Jesus before the
Sanhedrin

The Church of All Nations at the traditional site of the Garden of Gethsemane.

The Garden of Gethsemane looking west toward the city wall of old Jerusalem.

Inside the Garden of Gethsemane the olive trees and flowers provide a beautiful and tranquil scene.

Children in present-day Jerusalem playing a game in the street on the traditional Via Dolorosa.

The hill of Golgotha, or Place of the Skull, one of the traditional sites of Jesus' crucifixion.

The Garden Tomb is one site offered by tradition as the burial place of Jesus' body.

The Mount of Olives as viewed through one of the arched eastern entryways in the Temple Mount area.

Beautiful view of Mount Hermon from the ancient city-mound of Hazor in northern Galilee.

Model of ancient Megiddo.

The Valley of Jezreel (or Esdraelon) as viewed from Megiddo.

Part of Solomon's gate at ancient Megiddo.

Canaanite "high place" at Megiddo.

Well in the city of Sychar revered by tradition as Jacob's Well.

Sunrise ("eyelids of the morning" in Job 3:9).

Sunset over the Mediterranean Sea.

Roman pavement, or paving stones, on the main street at Caesarea.

Roman theater at Caesarea.

Dead Sea Scroll fragment.

The Dead Sea's high salt content makes it virtually impossible for a person to sink in its waters.

Aerial view of Herod's northern palace at Masada.

Large, extensive water cistern at Masada, Herod's mountain fortress.

Masada from the air with the "snake path" in the foreground.

The Parthenon, a temple dedicated to Athena, dominates the Acropolis in Athens, Greece.

The Acropolis at Athens.

The Erechtheum with the Porch of the Maidens on the Acropolis of ancient Athens.

The columns of the temple of Apollo at Corinth.

Mars Hill, where Paul preached his "unknown god" sermon, as viewed from the Acropolis of Athens.

The ruins of Corinth with the Acrocorinth in the distance.

The excavations at Corinth showing the shops in the Agora.

The re-erected marble façade of the Library of Celsus at ancient Ephesus.

Curetes Street in ancient Ephesus with the Library of Celsus in the background.

*The Great Theater of Ephesus with
the Arcadian Way in the background
leading to the ancient harbor.*

Cloesup of Ephesus Library.

Roadway into Ephesus.

The palace of Minos at Knossos on the island of Crete dates from the end of the Minoan Age.

Arabs winnowing grain in the ancient way with wooden winnowing forks.

An Arab shepherd tends his herd in the Judean hills.

Farmer plowing his field.

Fisherman casting his net on the Sea of Galilee

The blossoms and fruit of a pomegranate tree growing in Israel.

Olive trees provide fruit for the valuable olive oil of the Middle East.

A sycamore tree in Jericho which is like the one into which Zaccheus climbed to see Jesus.

Cyclamen is one of the flowers native to Israel.

Israel's Star of Bethlehem flower.

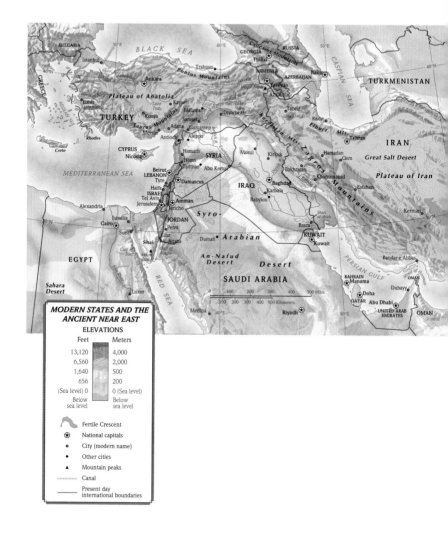

MODERN STATES AND THE ANCIENT NEAR EAST

ELEVATIONS

Feet	Meters
13,120	4,000
6,560	2,000
1,640	500
656	200
(Sea level) 0	0 (Sea level)
Below sea level	Below sea level

Fertile Crescent

⊛ National capitals

• City (modern name)

• Other cities

▲ Mountain peaks

.... Canal

——— Present day international boundaries

Appendix

With a Song in Your Heart

Songs of Christ's Birth

Songs of Christ's Death and Resurrection

Songs of Our Love for Christ

Songs of the Christian Life

Songs of Christ's Birth

Angels We Have Heard on High
Anonymous

Angels we have heard on high,
Sweetly singing o'er the plains,
And the mountains in reply
Echo back their joyous strains.
Refrain

Shepherds, why this jubilee?
Why your joyous strains prolong?
Say what may the tidings be,
Which inspire your heav'nly song?
Refrain

Come to Bethlehem, and see
Him whose birth the angels sing;
Come, adore on bended knee
Christ the Lord, the newborn King.
Refrain

See within a manger laid
Jesus, Lord of heav'n and earth!
Mary, Joseph, lend your aid,
With us sing our Savior's birth.
Refrain

Refrain
Glo - - - ria in excelsis Deo,
Glo - - - ria in excelsis Deo.

Away in a Manger

Anonymous; final stanza by John Thomas McFarland

Away in a manger, no crib for a bed,
The little Lord Jesus laid down His sweet head;
The stars in the bright sky looked down where He lay,
The little Lord Jesus, asleep on the hay.

The cattle are lowing, the Baby awakes,
But little Lord Jesus, no crying He makes.
I love Thee, Lord Jesus, look down from the sky,
And stay by my cradle till morning is nigh.

Be near me, Lord Jesus, I ask Thee to stay
Close by me forever, and love me, I pray.
Bless all the dear children in Thy tender care,
And fit us for heaven, to live with Thee there.

Hark! the Herald Angels Sing

By Charles Wesley

Hark! the herald angels sing, "Glory to the newborn
    King;
Peace on earth, and mercy mild, God and sinners
    reconciled!"
Joyful, all ye nations, rise, join the triumph of the skies;
With th' angelic host proclaim, "Christ is born in
    Bethlehem!"
Hark! the herald angels sing, "Glory to the newborn
    King."

Christ, by highest heav'n adored; Christ, the everlasting
    Lord!
Late in time behold Him come, offspring of the
    Virgin's womb:
Veiled in flesh the Godhead see; hail th' incarnate
    Deity,
Pleased as man with men to dwell, Jesus, our
    Emmanuel.
Hark! the herald angels sing, "Glory to the newborn
    King."

Hail the heav'n-born Prince of Peace! Hail the Sun of
    Righteousness!
Light and life to all He brings, ris'n with healing in His
    wings.
Mild He lays His glory by, born that man no more may
    die,
Born to raise the sons of earth, born to give them sec-
    ond birth.
Hark! the herald angels sing, "Glory to the newborn
    King."

Joy to the World!
By Isaac Watts

Joy to the world! the Lord is come; let earth receive
    her King;
Let ev'ry heart prepare Him room,
And heav'n and nature sing, and heav'n and nature
    sing,
And heav'n, and heav'n and nature sing.

Joy to the earth! the Savior reigns; let men their
    songs employ;
While fields and floods, rocks, hills, and plains
Repeat the sounding joy, repeat the sounding joy,
Repeat, repeat the sounding joy.

No more let sins and sorrows grow, nor thorns infest
    the ground;
He comes to make His blessings flow
Far as the curse is found, far as the curse is found,
Far as, far as the curse is found.

He rules the world with truth and grace, and makes
    the nations prove
The glories of His righteousness,
And wonders of His love, and wonders of His love,
And wonders, wonders of His love.

O Little Town of Bethlehem
By Philip Brooks

O little town of Bethlehem, how still we see thee lie!
Above thy deep and dreamless sleep the silent stars
    go by.
Yet in thy dark streets shineth the everlasting Light;
The hopes and fears of all the years are met in
    thee tonight.

For Christ is born of Mary, and gathered all above,
While mortals sleep, the angels keep their watch of
    wond'ring love,
O morning stars, together proclaim the holy birth!
And praises sing to God the King, and peace to
    men on earth.

How silently, how silently the wondrous gift is giv'n!
So God imparts to human hearts the blessings
    of His heav'n.
No ear may hear His coming, but in this world of sin,
Where meek souls will receive Him still the dear
    Christ enters in.

O holy Child of Bethlehem! Descend to us, we pray;
Cast out our sin, and enter in; be born in us today.
We hear the Christmas angels the great glad tidings tell;
O come to us, abide with us, our Lord Emmanuel.

Silent Night! Holy Night!

By Joseph Mohr; translated by John F. Young

Silent night, holy night, all is calm, all is bright
Round yon virgin mother and Child.
Holy infant so tender and mild,
Sleep in heavenly peace, sleep in heavenly peace.

Silent night, holy night, shepherds quake at the sight.
Glories stream from heaven afar,
Heavenly hosts sing alleluia;
Christ the Savior is born! Christ the Savior is born!

Silent night, holy night, Son of God, love's pure light
Radiant beams from Thy holy face, with the dawn of
    redeeming grace,
Jesus, Lord, at Thy birth, Jesus, Lord, at Thy birth.

Songs of Christ's Death and Resurrection

At the Cross
By Isaac Watts; refrain by Ralph E. Hudson

Alas! and did my Savior bleed? And did my
    Sov'reign die?
Would He devote that sacred head for sinners such as I!
Refrain

Was it for crimes that I have done He groaned upon
    the tree?
Amazing pity! grace unknown! And love beyond degree!
Refrain

Well might the sun in darkness hide and shut His
    glories in,
When Christ, the mighty Maker died for man the
    creature's sin.
Refrain

But drops of grief can ne'er repay the debt of love I
    owe:
Here, Lord, I give myself away—'tis all that I can do!
Refrain

Refrain
At the cross, at the cross where I first saw the light
And the burden of my heart rolled away—
It was there by faith I received my sight,
And now I am happy all the day!

Beneath the Cross of Jesus

By Elizabeth C. Clephane

Beneath the cross of Jesus I fain would take my stand—
The shadow of a mighty Rock within a weary land;
A home within the wilderness, a rest upon the way,
From the burning of the noontide heat, and the burden
    of the day.

Upon that cross of Jesus mine eye at times can see
The very dying form of One who suffered there for me;
And from my smitten heart with tears two wonders
    I confess—
The wonders of redeeming love and my unworthiness.

I take, O cross, thy shadow for my abiding place;
I ask no other sunshine than the sunshine of His face;
Content to let the world go by, to know no gain
    nor loss,
My sinful self my only shame, my glory all the cross.

Christ Arose

By Robert Lowry

Low in the grave He lay, Jesus my Savior!
Waiting the coming day, Jesus my Lord!
Refrain

Vainly they watch His bed, Jesus my Savior!
Vainly they seal the dead, Jesus my Lord!
Refrain

Death cannot keep his prey, Jesus my Savior!
He tore the bars away, Jesus my Lord!
Refrain

Refrain
Up from the grave He arose, with a mighty triumph
    o'er His foes;
He arose a Victor from the dark domain, and He lives
    forever with His saints to reign,
He arose! He arose! Hallelujah! Christ arose!

Hallelujah, What a Savior!
By Philip P. Bliss

"Man of Sorrows!" what a name for the Son of God,
who came
Ruined sinners to reclaim! Hallelujah, what a Savior!

Bearing shame and scoffing rude, in my place
condemned He stood—
Sealed my pardon with His blood: Hallelujah,
what a Savior!

Guilty, vile and helpless we, spotless Lamb of God
was He;
Full atonement! can it be? Hallelujah, what a Savior!

Lifted up was He to die, "It is finished!" was His cry;
Now in heav'n exalted high: Hallelujah, what a Savior!

When He comes, our glorious King, all His ransomed
home to bring,
Then anew this song we'll sing: Hallelujah, what a
Savior!

Tell Me the Story of Jesus
By Fanny J. Crosby

Tell me the story of Jesus, write on my heart
 every word;
Tell me the story most precious, sweetest that ever
 was heard.
Tell how the angels in chorus sang as they welcomed
 His birth,
"Glory to God in the highest! Peace and good tidings
 to earth."
Refrain

Fasting alone in the desert, tell of the days that are past,
How for our sins He was tempted, yet was
 triumphant at last.
Tell of the years of His labor, tell of the sorrow
 He bore,
He was despised and afflicted, homeless, rejected
 and poor.
Refrain

Tell of the cross where they nailed Him, writhing in
 anguish and pain;
Tell of the grave where they laid Him, tell how He
 liveth again.
Love in that story so tender, clearer than ever I see:
Stay let me weep while you whisper, love paid the
 ransom for me.
Refrain

Refrain
Tell me the story of Jesus, write on my heart
 every word;
Tell me the story most precious, sweetest that ever
 was heard.

Were You There?

Anonymous

Were you there when they crucified my Lord?
Were you there when they crucified my Lord?
O!—Sometimes it causes me to tremble,
　　tremble, tremble!
Were you there when they crucified my Lord?

Were you there when they nailed Him to the tree?
Were you there when they nailed Him to the tree?
O!—Sometimes it causes me to tremble,
　　tremble, tremble!
Were you there when they nailed Him to the tree?

Were you there when they laid Him in the tomb?
Were you there when they laid Him in the tomb?
O!—Sometimes it causes me to tremble,
　　tremble, tremble!
Were you there when they laid Him in the tomb?

Were you there when He rose up from the dead?
Were you there when He rose up from the dead?
O!—Sometimes I feel like shouting glory, glory, glory!
Were you there when He rose up from the dead?

When I Survey the Wondrous Cross
By Isaac Watts

When I survey the wondrous cross on which the Prince
of glory died,
My richest gain I count but loss, and pour contempt
on all my pride.

Forbid it, Lord, that I should boast, save in the death of
Christ, my God;
All the vain things that charm me most—I sacrifice
them to His blood.

See, from His head, His hands, His feet, sorrow and
love flow mingled down;
Did e'er such love and sorrow meet, or thorns compose
so rich a crown?

Were the whole realm of nature mine, that were a
present far too small:
Love so amazing, so divine, demands my soul, my life,
my all.

Songs of Our Love for Christ

Blessed Be the Name
By William H. Clark; refrain by Ralph E. Hudson

All praise to Him who reigns above in
    majesty supreme,
Who gave His Son for man to die, that He might
    man redeem!
Refrain

His name above all names shall stand, exalted more
    and more,
At God the Father's own right hand, where angel
    hosts adore.
Refrain

His name shall be the Counselor, the mighty Prince
    of Peace,
Of all earth's kingdoms Conqueror, whose reign shall
    never cease.
Refrain

Refrain
Blessed be the name, blessed be the name, blessed be
    the name of the Lord;
Blessed be the name, blessed be the name, blessed be
    the name of the Lord.

Fairest Lord Jesus

Anonymous

Fairest Lord Jesus, Ruler of all nature, O Thou of God
and man the Son:
Thee will I cherish, Thee will I honor, Thou my soul's
glory, joy, and crown.

Fair are the meadows, fairer still the woodlands, robed
in the blooming garb of spring:
Jesus is fairer, Jesus is purer, who makes the woeful
heart to sing.

Fair is the sunshine, fairer still the moonlight, and all
the twinkling starry host:
Jesus shines brighter, Jesus shines purer than all the
angels heaven can boast.

Beautiful Savior! Lord of the nations! Son of God and
Son of Man!
Glory and honor, praise, adoration, now and forever-
more be Thine!

Holy, Holy, Holy
By Reginald Heber

Holy, holy, holy! Lord God Almighty! Early in the
morning our song shall rise to Thee;
Holy, holy, holy! merciful and mighty! God in
three Persons, blessed Trinity!

Holy, holy, holy! all the saints adore Thee, casting
down their golden crowns around the glassy sea;
Cherubim and seraphim falling down before Thee,
which wert and art and evermore shalt be.

Holy, holy, holy! though the darkness hide Thee,
though the eye of sinful man Thy glory may
not see;
Only Thou art holy—there is none beside Thee,
perfect in pow'r, in love and purity.

Holy, holy, holy! Lord God Almighty! All Thy works
shall praise Thy name in earth and sky and sea;
Holy, holy, holy! merciful and mighty! God in three
Persons, blessed Trinity!

I Love to Tell the Story
By A. Catherine Hankey

I love to tell the story of unseen things above,
  of Jesus and His glory, of Jesus and His love;
I love to tell the story because I know 'tis true, it
  satisfies my longings as nothing else can do.
Refrain

I love to tell the story— 'tis pleasant to repeat what
  seems, each time I tell it, more wonderfully sweet;
I love to tell the story, for some have never heard the
  message of salvation from God's own holy Word.
Refrain

I love to tell the story, for those who know it best seem
  hungering and thirsting to hear it like the rest;
And when in scenes of glory I sing the new, new song,
  'twill be the old, old story that I have loved so long.
Refrain

Refrain
I love to tell the story! 'Twill be my theme in glory—
  to tell the old, old story of Jesus and His love.

Jesus Paid It All
By Elvina M. Hall

I hear the Savior say, "Thy strength indeed is small!
Child of weakness, watch and pray, find in Me thine all
   in all."
Refrain

Lord, now indeed I find Thy pow'r, and Thine alone,
Can change the leper's spots and melt the heart
   of stone.
Refrain

For nothing good have I whereby Thy grace to claim—
I'll wash my garments white in the blood of
   Calv'ry's Lamb.
Refrain

And when before the throne I stand in Him complete,
"Jesus died my soul to save," my lips shall still repeat.
Refrain

Refrain
Jesus paid it all, all to Him I owe;
Sin had left a crimson stain—He washed it white
   as snow.

More About Jesus

By Eliza E. Hewitt

More about Jesus would I know, more of His grace to
others show,
More of His saving fullness see, more of His love who
died for me.
Refrain

More about Jesus let me learn, more of His holy
will discern;
Spirit of God, my teacher be, showing the things of
Christ to me.
Refrain

More about Jesus; in His Word, holding communion
with my Lord,
Hearing His voice in ev'ry line, making each faithful
saying mine.
Refrain

More about Jesus on His throne, riches in glory all
His own,
More of His kingdom's sure increase, more of His
coming—Prince of Peace.
Refrain

Refrain
More, more about Jesus, more, more about Jesus;
More of His saving fullness see, more of His love
who died for me!

Must Jesus Bear the Cross Alone?

By Thomas Shepherd and others

Must Jesus bear the cross alone and all the world
  go free?
No, there's a cross for ev'ryone, and there's a cross
  for me.

The consecrated cross I'll bear till death shall set
  me free,
And then go home my crown to wear, for there's a
  crown for me.

Upon the crystal pavement, down at Jesus' pierced feet,
Joyful I'll cast my golden crown and His dear
  name repeat.

O precious cross! O glorious crown! O resurrection day!
Ye angels from the stars come down and bear my
  soul away.

My Jesus, I Love Thee
By William R. Featherston

My Jesus, I love Thee, I know Thou art mine—
For Thee all the follies of sin I resign;
My gracious Redeemer, my Savior art Thou:
If ever I loved Thee, my Jesus 'tis now.

I love Thee because Thou hast first loved me
And purchased my pardon on Calvary's tree;
I love Thee for wearing the thorns on Thy brow:
If ever I loved Thee, my Jesus 'tis now.

I'll love Thee in life, I will love Thee in death,
And praise Thee as long as Thou lendest me breath;
And say when the death-dew lies cold on my brow,
"If ever I loved Thee, my Jesus 'tis now."

In mansions of glory and endless delight,
I'll ever adore Thee in heaven so bright;
I'll sing with the glittering crown on my brow,
"If ever I loved Thee, my Jesus 'tis now."

O for a Thousand Tongues
By Charles Wesley

O for a thousand tongues to sing My great redeemer's
    praise,
The glories of My God and King, the triumphs of His
    grace.

Jesus! the name that charms our fears, that bids our sor-
    rows cease,
'Tis music in the sinner's ears, 'tis life and health and
    peace.

He breaks the power of canceled sin, He sets the pris-
    oner free;
His blood can make the foulest clean; His blood availed
    for me.

Hear Him, ye deaf; His praise, ye dumb, your loosened
    tongues employ;
Ye blind, behold your Savior come; and leap, ye lame,
    for joy.

My gracious Master and my God, assist me to pro-
    claim,
To spread thro' all the earth abroad, the honors of Thy
    name.

Songs of the Christian Life

All the Way My Savior Leads Me
By Fanny J. Crosby

All the way me Savior leads me; what have I to ask
   beside?
Can I doubt His tender mercy, who thro' life has been
   my guide?
Heav'nly peace, divinest comfort, here by faith in Him
   to dwell!
For I know whate'er befall me, Jesus doeth all
   things well;
For I know whate'er befall me, Jesus doeth all
   things well.

All the way my Savior leads me; cheers each winding
   path I tread,
Gives me grace for ev'ry trial, feeds me with the
   living bread:
Though my weary steps may falter, and my soul athirst
   may be,
Gushing from the Rock before me, Lo! a spring of joy
   I see;
Gushing from the Rock before me, Lo! a spring of joy
   I see.

All the way my Savior leads me; oh, the fullness of
    His love!
Perfect rest to me is promised in my Father's
    house above:
When my spirit, clothed immortal, wings its flight to
    realms of day,
This my song thru endless ages: Jesus led me all
    the way;
This my song thru endless ages: Jesus led me all the
    way.

Amazing Grace

By John Newton; final stanza by John P. Rees

Amazing grace! how sweet the sound—that saved a
    wretch like me!
I once was lost but now am found, was blind but
    now I see.

'Twas grace that taught my heart to fear, and grace my
    fears relieved;
How precious did that grace appear the hour I
    first believed.

The Lord has promised good to me, His word my hope
    secures;
He will my shield and portion be as long as
    life endures.

Thru many dangers, toils and snares, I have
    already come;
'Tis grace hath brought me safe thus far, and grace will
    lead me home.

When we've been there ten thousand years, bright shin-
    ing as the sun,
We've no less days to sing God's praise than when we'd
    first begun.

Blessed Assurance
By Fanny J. Crosby

Blessed assurance, Jesus is mine! O what a foretaste of
glory divine!
Heir of salvation, purchase of God, born of His Spirit,
washed in His blood.
Refrain

Perfect submission, perfect delight! Visions of rapture
now burst on my sight;
Angels descending bring from above echoes of mercy,
whispers of love.
Refrain

Perfect submission—all is at rest, I in my Savior am
happy and blest;
Watching and waiting, looking above, filled with His
goodness, lost in His love.
Refrain

Refrain
This is my story, this is my song, praising my Savior all
the day long;
This is my story, this is my song, praising my Savior all
the day long.

Blest Be the Tie That Binds

By John Fawcett

Blest be the tie that binds our hearts in Christian love;
The fellowship of kindred minds is like to that above.

Before our Father's throne we pour our ardent prayers;
Our fears, our hopes, our aims are one, our comforts
and our cares.

When we asunder part, it gives us inward pain;
But we shall still be joined in heart, and hope to
meet again.

Day by Day

By Carolina Sandell Berg; translated by Andrew L. Skoog

Day by day and with each passing moment, strength I
find to meet my trials here;
Trusting in my Father's wise bestowment, I've no cause
for worry or for fear.
He whose heart is kind beyond all measure gives unto
each day what He deems best—
Lovingly, its part of pain and pleasure, mingling toil
with peace and rest.

Every day the Lord Himself is near me with a special
mercy for each hour;
All my cares He fain would bear, and cheer me, He
whose name is Counselor and Pow'r.
The protection of His child and treasure is a charge
that on Himself He laid;
"As your days, your strength shall be in measure," this
the pledge to me He made.

Help me then in ev'ry tribulation so to trust Thy
promises, O Lord,
That I lose not faith's sweet consolation offered me
within Thy holy Word.
Help me, Lord, when toil and trouble meeting, e'er to
take, as from a father's hand,
One by one, the days, the moments fleeting, till I reach
the promised land.

Face to Face
By Carrie E. Breck

Face to face with Christ my Savior, face to face—what
    will it be—
When with rapture I behold Him, Jesus Christ who
    died for me?
Refrain

Only faintly now I see Him, with the darkling veil
    between;
But a blessed day is coming when His glory shall
    be seen.
Refrain

What rejoicing in His presence when are banished grief
    and pain;
When the crooked ways are straightened and the dark
    things shall be plain.
Refrain

Face to face! O blissful moment! Face to face—to see
    and know;
Face to face with my Redeemer, Jesus Christ who loves
    me so.
Refrain

Refrain
Face to face I shall behold Him, far beyond the
    starry sky;
Face to face in all His glory, I shall see Him by and by.

Have Thine Own Way, Lord

By Adelaide A. Pollard

Have Thine own way, Lord! Have Thine own way!
    Thou art the Potter, I am the clay.
Mold me and make me after Thy will, while I am
    waiting, yielded and still.

Have Thine own way, Lord! Have Thine own way!
    Search me and try me, Master today!
Whiter than snow, Lord, wash me just now, as in Thy
    presence humbly I bow.

Have Thine own way, Lord! Have Thine own way!
    Wounded and weary, help me I pray!
Power—all power—surely is Thine! Touch me and heal
    me, Savior divine!

Have Thine own way, Lord! Have Thine own way!
    Hold o'er my being absolute sway!
Fill with Thy Spirit till all shall see Christ only, always,
    living in me!

It Is Well with My Soul
By Horatio G. Spafford

When peace like a river attendeth my way, when sorrows like sea-billows roll;
Whatever my lot, Thou hast taught me to say, "It is
well, it is well with my soul."
Refrain

Though Satan should buffet, though trials should
come, let this blest assurance control,
That Christ has regarded my helpless estate, and hath
shed His own blood for my soul.
Refrain

My sin—O the bliss of this glorious thought, my sin—
not in part but the whole,
Is nailed to the cross and I bear it no more, praise the
Lord, praise the Lord, O my soul!
Refrain

And, Lord, haste the day when the faith shall be sight,
the clouds be rolled back as a scroll,
The trump shall resound and the Lord shall descend,
"Even so"—it is well with my soul.
Refrain

Refrain
It is well (It is well) with my soul (with my soul),
It is well, it is well with my soul.

Nearer, My God, to Thee

By Sarah F. Adams

Nearer, my God, to Thee, Nearer to Thee! E'en though
    it be a cross that raiseth me;
Still all my song shall be, nearer, my God, to Thee,
    nearer, my God, to Thee, nearer to Thee.

Though like the wanderer, the sun gone down,
    darkness be over me, my rest a stone;
Yet in my dreams I'd be nearer, my God, to Thee,
    nearer, my God, to Thee, nearer to Thee.

There let the way appear steps unto heav'n; all that
    Thou sendest me in mercy giv'n;
Angels to beckon me nearer, my God, to Thee, nearer,
    my God, to Thee, nearer to Thee.

Then, with my waking thoughts bright with Thy
    praise, out of my stony griefs, Bethel I'll raise;
So by my woes to be nearer, my God, to Thee, nearer,
    my God, to Thee, nearer to Thee.

Or if on joyful wing, cleaving the sky, sun, moon, and
    stars forgot, upward I fly,
Still all my song shall be nearer, my God, to Thee,
    nearer, my God, to Thee, nearer to Thee.

Sweet Hour of Prayer
By William W. Walford

Sweet hour of prayer, sweet hour of prayer, that calls
    me from a world of care,
And bids me at my Father's throne make all my wants
    and wishes known:
In seasons of distress and grief my soul has often found
    relief,
And oft escaped the tempter's snare by thy return, sweet
    hour of prayer.

Sweet hour of prayer, sweet hour of prayer, thy wings
    shall my petition bear
To Him whose truth and faithfulness engage the
    waiting soul to bless:
And since He bids me seek His face, believe His Word,
    and trust His grace,
I'll cast on Him my ev'ry care, and wait for thee, sweet
    hour of prayer.

Take Time to Be Holy
By William D. Longstaff

Take time to be holy, speak oft with thy Lord; abide
    in Him always, and feed on His Word.
Make friends of God's children; help those who are
    weak; forgetting in nothing His blessing to seek.

Take time to be holy, the world rushes on; much time
    spend in secret with Jesus alone;
By looking to Jesus, like Him thou shalt be; thy friends
    in thy conduct His likeness shall see.

Take time to be holy, let Him be thy guide, and run
    not before Him whatever betide;
In joy or in sorrow still follow thy Lord, and, looking
    to Jesus, still trust in His Word.

Take time to be holy, be calm in thy soul; each thought
    and each motive beneath His control;
Thus led by His Spirit to fountains of love, thou soon
    shalt be fitted for service above.

Under His Wings

By William O. Cushing

Under His wings I am safely abiding, though the night
    deepens and tempests are wild;
Still I can trust Him, I know He will keep me, He has
    redeemed me and I am His child.
Refrain

Under His wings, what a refuge in sorrow! How the
    heart yearningly turns to His rest!
Often when earth has no balm for my healing, there I
    find comfort and there I am blest.
Refrain

Under His wings, O what precious enjoyment! There
    will I hide till life's trials are o'er;
Sheltered, protected, no evil can harm me, resting in
    Jesus I'm safe evermore.
Refrain

Refrain
Under His wings, under His wings, Who from His love
    can sever?
Under His wings my soul shall abide, safely
    abide forever.

What a Friend We Have in Jesus
By Joseph M. Scriven

What a Friend we have in Jesus, all our sins and griefs
    to bear!
What a privilege to carry everything to God in prayer!
O what peace we often forfeit, O what needless pain
    we bear,
All because we do not carry everything to God in
    prayer!

Have we trials and temptations? Is there trouble
    anywhere?
We should never be discouraged, take it to the
    Lord in prayer.
Can we find a friend so faithful who will all our
    sorrows share?
Jesus knows our every weakness, take it to the
    Lord in prayer.

Are we weak and heavy-laden, cumbered with a load of
    care?
Precious Savior, still our Refuge—take it to the
    Lord in prayer.
Do thy friends despise, forsake thee? Take it to the
    Lord in prayer;
In His arms He'll take and shield thee, thou wilt find a
    solace there.

Recommended Reading List

The following books are an excellent source of additional information on the land of Israel.

THE ARCHAEOLOGY AND GEOGRAPHY OF ISRAEL

Beitzel, Barry J. *The Moody Atlas of Bible Lands.* Chicago: Moody Press, 1985.

Laney, J. Carl. *Baker's Concise Bible Atlas.* Grand Rapids: Baker Book House, 1988.

Rasmussen, Carl G. *NIV Atlas of the Bible.* Grand Rapids: Zondervan Publishing House, 1989.

Shanks, Hershel, and Mazar, Benjamin, eds. *Recent Archaeology in the Land of Israel.* Washington, D.C.: Biblical Archaeology Society, 1984.

Smith, Marsha A. Ellis. *Holman Book of Biblical Charts, Maps, and Reconstructions.* Nashville: Broadman & Holman Publishers, 1993.

THE HISTORY OF ISRAEL

Merrill, Eugene H. *Kingdom of Priests: A History of Old Testament Israel.* Grand Rapids: Baker Book House, 1987.

Pentecost, J. Dwight. *The Words and Works of Jesus Christ: A Study in the Life of Christ.* Grand Rapids: Zondervan Publishing House, 1981.

Collins, Larry, and Lapierre, Dominique. *O Jerusalem!* London: Collins Publishing, 1982.

HISTORICAL FICTION RELATED TO ISRAEL

Arthur, Kay. *Israel, My Beloved.* Eugene, Oreg.: Harvest House Publishers, 1996.

Michener, James A. *The Source.* New York: Random House, 1965.

Thoene, Bodie. *The Gates of Zion.* The Zion Chronicles. Minneapolis: Bethany House Publishers, 1986.

———. *A Daughter of Zion.* The Zion Chronicles. Minneapolis: Bethany House Publishers, 1987.

———. *The Return to Zion.* The Zion Chronicles. Minneapolis: Bethany House Publishers, 1987.

———. *A Light in Zion.* The Zion Chronicles. Minneapolis: Bethany House Publishers, 1988.

———. *The Key to Zion.* The Zion Chronicles. Minneapolis: Bethany House Publishers, 1988.

ROLL # _____

1	
2	
3	
4	
5	
6	
7	
8	
9	
10	
11	
12	
13	
14	
15	
16	
17	
18	
19	
20	
21	
22	
23	
24	
25	
26	
27	
28	
29	
30	
31	
32	
34	
35	
36	

ROLL # _____

1	
2	
3	
4	
5	
6	
7	
8	
9	
10	
11	
12	
13	
14	
15	
16	
17	
18	
19	
20	
21	
22	
23	
24	
25	
26	
27	
28	
29	
30	
31	
32	
34	
35	
36	

ROLL # _____

1	
2	
3	
4	
5	
6	
7	
8	
9	
10	
11	
12	
13	
14	
15	
16	
17	
18	
19	
20	
21	
22	
23	
24	
25	
26	
27	
28	
29	
30	
31	
32	
34	
35	
36	

ROLL # _____

1	
2	
3	
4	
5	
6	
7	
8	
9	
10	
11	
12	
13	
14	
15	
16	
17	
18	
19	
20	
21	
22	
23	
24	
25	
26	
27	
28	
29	
30	
31	
32	
34	
35	
36	

ROLL # _____

1 _____
2 _____
3 _____
4 _____
5 _____
6 _____
7 _____
8 _____
9 _____
10 _____
11 _____
12 _____
13 _____
14 _____
15 _____
16 _____
17 _____
18 _____
19 _____
20 _____
21 _____
22 _____
23 _____
24 _____
25 _____
26 _____
27 _____
28 _____
29 _____
30 _____
31 _____
32 _____
34 _____
35 _____
36 _____

ROLL # _____

1 _____
2 _____
3 _____
4 _____
5 _____
6 _____
7 _____
8 _____
9 _____
10 _____
11 _____
12 _____
13 _____
14 _____
15 _____
16 _____
17 _____
18 _____
19 _____
20 _____
21 _____
22 _____
23 _____
24 _____
25 _____
26 _____
27 _____
28 _____
29 _____
30 _____
31 _____
32 _____
34 _____
35 _____
36 _____

ROLL # _____

1	
2	
3	
4	
5	
6	
7	
8	
9	
10	
11	
12	
13	
14	
15	
16	
17	
18	
19	
20	
21	
22	
23	
24	
25	
26	
27	
28	
29	
30	
31	
32	
34	
35	
36	

ROLL # _____

1	
2	
3	
4	
5	
6	
7	
8	
9	
10	
11	
12	
13	
14	
15	
16	
17	
18	
19	
20	
21	
22	
23	
24	
25	
26	
27	
28	
29	
30	
31	
32	
34	
35	
36	

Tour Notes

Tour Notes

Tour Notes

Tour Notes